W9-BUO-467

CLOSE
QUARTERS

A WOMAN'S GUIDE
TO LIVING AND WORKING
IN MASCULINE ENVIRONMENTS

Capt. Tuuli Messer-Bookman

4880 Lower Valley Road, Atglen, Pennsylvania 19310

Schiffer Books are available at special discounts for bulk purchases for sales promotions or premiums. Special editions, including personalized covers, corporate imprints, and excerpts can be created in large quantities for special needs. For more information contact the publisher:

Schiffer Publishing Ltd.
4880 Lower Valley Road
Atglen, PA 19310
Phone: (610) 593-1777
Fax: (610) 593-2002
E-mail: Info@schifferbooks.com

For the largest selection of fine books on this and related subjects, please visit our web site at

www.schifferbooks.com

We are always looking for people to write books on new and related subjects. If you have an idea for a book please contact us at the above address.

This book may be purchased from the publisher. Include $5.00 for shipping. Please try your bookstore first. You may write for a free catalog.

In Europe, Schiffer books are distributed by
Bushwood Books
6 Marksbury Ave.
Kew Gardens
Surrey TW9 4JF England
Phone: 44 (0) 20 8392 8585; Fax: 44 (0) 20 8392 9876
E-mail: info@bushwoodbooks.co.uk
Website: www.bushwoodbooks.co.uk

Designed by Stephanie Daugherty
Type set in Lydian BT/Zurich BT

ISBN: 978-0-7643-3631-7
Printed in the United States

Dedication

For my parents,
Sidney and Laila Messer

Acknowledgements

I'd like to thank my colleague, Dave Coleman, whose research inspired me and gave me the impetus to write this book. I also recognize my colleagues, Capt. Paul Leyda and Capt. Peter Hayes, for their support and advice during the initial stages of this work. I thank my friend, Pat Winter, for letting me share her experiences working in the automotive industry. Our campus Chief of Police, Dr. Roseann Richard, graciously related her experiences and doctoral dissertation with me, which added breadth and depth to the manuscript. Perspectives on being a woman in the military from former U.S. Marine Mercy Wright added another dimension to the book. My longtime friend, law school buddy, and fellow Kings Pointer, Keith Gillette, Esq., offered valuable legal advice. I acknowledge California Maritime Academy cadets Michael J. Durnan, Stephen C. Coutts, and Philomena "Phil" Sulzen, whose delightful artwork is featured in the book. My editor, Elizabeth Brierly, imparted invaluable advice, and I truly appreciate her exacting eye. Most importantly, I thank my wonderful husband, Barry, for encouraging me, bringing me tea, and rubbing my shoulders when I would stay up all night working on this book.

Contents

Foreword

Captain Tuuli Messer-Bookman has written a fantastic guide for young people in her hard hitting *Close Quarters — A Woman's Guide to Living and Working in Masculine Environments*. More than just a string of anecdotal memories, Tuuli lays it out on the line in providing relevant advice for both genders, in managing their careers and relationships.

Written mainly for women entering the maritime industry, Tuuli's insight, earned through her experiences as master mariner, professor and lawyer, uniquely qualify her as an expert helping young professionals navigate through the reefs and shoals of their careers. In *It All Matters: How to Behave*, she stresses the importance "of giving yourself every advantage" and how "classy behavior" shapes lasting perceptions and builds positive reputations that serve professionals throughout their careers.

Never lacking for a good story, Captain Messer-Bookman takes us through the tough challenges she faced entering the workforce and dealing with being a token female. Her chapter *Improvise—Adapt—Overcome: Quitting My First Job* explains how she developed the wisdom to know when it is time to move on from a job she hated. In short order, she moves on to describe the nontraditional workplace and how to sense when the social balance is skewed. She provides great insight into how to work successfully in a masculine environment and how to start off on the right foot.

Tuuli's final thoughts are a great pep talk that takes the reader through the steps of planning a successful career. True to her personality, she emphasizes the need to be passionate about life, as well as one's career. The insight and reflection shown in *Close Quarters* are a hallmark of her alma mater and ring true its motto: *Acta non Verba*: Deeds not Words!

Captain Jeff Flumignan
U. S. Maritime Service
U. S. Merchant Marine Academy

Introduction

"Alone at a Table" by Stephen C. Coutts

♂♀♂

Greetings ladies!

You just noticed I used the word "ladies" to address you. There is a distinction (even according to a dictionary) between ladies and women. It is my hope that you will choose to act as ladies, not just women, no matter what your circumstances, socioeconomic background, training, education, or work environment.

My father once told me, "Only fools have to learn from their own mistakes." By sharing my mistakes and perspectives with you, I hope to save you, as well as your co-workers, a good deal of drama, angst, and heartache. The advice I offer is probably advice your mother didn't give you, only because she couldn't. Most likely, given the timing of your mother's working years and the social climate at the time, she didn't have the dizzying array of opportunities you do. She may have chosen a more traditional profession or been a stay-at-home mom, which is an honorable, needed, and demanding position.

It has been my experience working in a "man's world" all my life, that acting as a lady has propelled me further, and with less drama, than trying to be "one of the guys." In the beginning, I tried being one of the guys. I learned how to swagger, and swear, and hook my thumbs in my belt loops. I tried to get interested in spectator sports. All of that turned out to be utterly ineffective. None of those behaviors ingratiated me with my male colleagues. In fact, the usual effect was to further alienate me and leave me treading water in a social "no man's land" somewhere between female and male—and doing neither well. In short, it didn't work. That took me several years to figure out. Once I relaxed and just let myself be me, everything smoothed out.

Former U.S. Marine Mercy Wright has a similar perspective:

> I personally believe that with an open mind, being true to oneself in all respects (goals, ambitions, dreams, and desires) a woman is just as powerful still being a woman in a respectful and professional way, even when surrounded by men....I joined the Marine Corps....for the pride of accomplishment knowing that I could train the exact same way a man did and feel his equal, yet not to think, behave, or act like a man. Not that anything is wrong with that, but a man is a man and a woman is a woman, and there are differences.[1]

Let me tell you a little bit about myself and share the circumstances and experiences that are the foundation of the opinions I am about to share with you. I am a 1986 graduate of the U.S. Merchant Marine Academy at Kings Point, New York, usually referred to as "Kings Point" or sometimes, "the Point." (When we were in trouble and restricted to campus, we called it "the Farm.")

Kings Point is one of five federal service academies. Unlike the Military, Navy, Air Force, and Coast Guard academies, Kings Point graduates are not required to go into active duty service status upon graduation. Kings Point trains the officers who operate the nation's merchant ships. Deep-sea merchant ships are the cargo ships that carry goods to and from the United States and abroad. Much of what we eat, wear, drive, and pump into our cars is carried to this country on merchant vessels. Merchant vessels also include ferries, tugs, cruise ships, research vessels, fishing boats, and other non-recreational working vessels.

Kings Point graduates are required to take commissions in the U.S. Naval Reserve (or some other service). We have a service obligation, monitored by the U.S. Maritime Administration, to work in the maritime industry for at least five years. We are graduated with bachelor's degrees in marine transportation or marine engineering, or both.

After rigorous examinations, physicals, and background checks, the U.S. Coast Guard licenses us to work aboard U.S.-flagged vessels as deck or engineering officers, similar to the Federal Aviation Administration's licensing of airplane pilots.

Some Kings Point graduates choose to serve as active-duty officers in the navy or another service. Some go to sea or work on inland waters on "brown water" vessels such as ferries, tugs, and dredges. Some work ashore in maritime-related industries. A few proceed directly to graduate school.

In the 1980s the academy's corps of midshipmen was just barely above 10 percent female. The percentage of female midshipmen has not significantly changed. When I was a cadet, no women were teaching any of the professional, license-related courses, and there were no female faculty in uniform, as we midshipmen were. We did, however, have a female faculty member who was to act as our mentor.

As nice as she was, most of us didn't go to her for advice, because she had not attended an academy and had never been to sea. It wasn't the school's fault that there were no female role models in the 1980s. Women had been allowed into the maritime academies only since the mid-1970s. In 1982, when I entered Kings Point, there were not yet enough senior female officers to even begin to form a candidate pool from which to hire female faculty. This has changed. Now almost every academy employs female faculty in uniform.

I chose Kings Point because I wanted to work at sea. Although I was raised on a sailboat, neither of my parents had any commercial maritime background, nor had they ever heard of the U.S. Merchant Marine Academy.

Upon graduation, I had a bachelor's degree in marine transportation, a commission as an ensign in the U.S. Naval Reserve, and an unlimited-tonnage third mate's license from the U.S. Coast Guard. Third mates are the lowest-ranking deck officers aboard merchant ships.

Since then, I have worked aboard all sorts of vessels as I worked my way up the ranks. Now I hold the U.S. Coast Guard's highest commercial license: master, unlimited tonnage (upon oceans), which licenses me to command cargo vessels of any tonnage, upon any waters. I have never served aboard a naval vessel, but I have sailed in convoy and worked, under military contract, in concert with the navy many times. I maintained my U.S. Naval Reserve commission for twenty years, and attained the rank of Lieutenant Commander before separating.

When I started going to sea, I worked through a maritime union. Working through a union allowed me to be nimble and virtually unisex when seeking work, because mariners were shipped out based solely on union seniority. To the union, I was just a license with a number. Often a ship would only be notified that an officer "T. Messer" had been shipped, and the crew had no idea I was female. My appearance at the gangway was usually met with surprise and either a smile or a frown, but it never failed to evoke a reaction.

I worked mostly aboard tankers, carrying both clean (e.g., gasoline) and dirty (e.g., crude oil) cargos. I also worked aboard a car carrier, a surveillance ship, various container ships, a break-bulk cargo ship carrying bagged corn to Africa, and a semi-submersible stationed at Diego Garcia, an island in the Indian Ocean. I crewed on a fish-processor vessel from the Bering Sea to Seattle, and on a small landing craft (on which, with only three men aboard, I had to share a cabin with one of them) on a two-month trip from Oregon, through the Panama Canal, to the Bahamas.

I have sailed the North and South Pacific, the North and South Atlantic, and the Indian oceans. I have visited every continent except Antarctica. I have had dozens of adventures visiting exotic locales, including Easter Island in the South Pacific, Ascension Island in the Atlantic, Hong Kong, Durban, Fiji, Mozambique, Wake Island, Rio de Janeiro, Palmyra Atoll, Singapore, and the Straits of Magellan, to name just a few.

I have sailed well over 300,000 miles at sea as a licensed officer. I have sailed with all types of crews, from the most ragtag to the most professional. I never sailed with another female officer aboard, though I did sail occasionally with unlicensed female crew members.

After going to sea, I went to law school, where I earned a Juris Doctor degree. I passed the California State Bar exam, though I had no desire to earn a living practicing law. I do testify occasionally as an expert witness, and I enjoy exploring various aspects of the law, especially admiralty and constitutional law. As of this writing, I am employed as a tenured, full professor at the California Maritime Academy, where I have taught since 1995.

I have worked with hundreds of cadets, of both sexes and of every possible color and persuasion. Recognize that what follows are my own opinions and they do not reflect the positions of the California Maritime Academy, the U.S. Merchant Marine Academy, or anyone else. Actually, I fully expect that my views will be contrary to the policies and practices of many institutions.

In my experience, every school I attended and every company that I worked for did the best it could to accommodate the shifting demographics of their student bodies and work forces. Adapting to shifting social perceptions and expectations takes time, and cannot be rushed without generating push-back and resentment. I realized and accepted this, and as a result, had a mostly happy time living and working in very masculine environments. Many of my worst experiences, which really weren't that bad, came during my years at Kings Point—not my time in the work world.

By modern, politically correct standards, my advice may be considered uncomfortably forthright. Ultimately, I hope it will enhance your career and make you, and those who work with you, happier and more at ease. These are strictly my opinions borne of my experiences and observations, and augmented by interviews I've conducted with women in other male-dominated professions and industries. Your experiences assuredly will be different from mine, but I hope just as rewarding.

1

The Token Female:
Landing My First Job

"Weren't a Girl" by Michael J. Durnan

♂♀♂

I n the summer of 1986, Kings Point was abuzz with several hundred senior midshipmen all competing for employment. We had been warned that seagoing jobs were scarce, so almost everyone was applying for every employment opportunity, ashore or afloat. Some midshipmen would consider only jobs as officers; others, like me, were not so picky. I just wanted a job.

At Kings Point, there was a job-posting board on zero-deck, which was a wide underground hallway that housed the barber shop, post office, and bookstore, and connected the academy's barracks and cafeteria. When a job opportunity arrived, it was posted on the board on zero-deck. Some offered lucrative seagoing positions and others were shore-based jobs. There were also weekend jobs posted there, such as shoveling snow, raking leaves, or jobs as waiters or bartenders for wealthy people's private soirées.

During our final semester, I noticed my classmates attending presentations on résumé preparation, and collecting business cards at various academy functions. I had always assumed I would just join a union and go to sea as a third officer—but when a job with Shell Oil headquarters in Houston, Texas appeared on the board, everything changed. It was a dream job. It paid well, and was secure and prestigious. It seemed as though everyone wanted it.

My boyfriend at the time, a soft-spoken engineering officer from Mississippi, tried to convince me that I really didn't have what it takes to go to sea and that I should consider a shore-side job. I bristled at this like a stepped-on cat, because I had evidence to the contrary.

Part of our training as midshipmen required we spend a year at sea on commercial cargo ships. I had received very good scores on my sea-year assignments and had enjoyed my seagoing experiences immensely. I wasn't used to people telling me what I couldn't or shouldn't do, so I didn't like being told I was "unfit" to go to sea, especially given all the positive feedback I had received from senior officers.

But my boyfriend was older than I was, had graduated Kings Point, and had spent a few years at sea, so I believed him. I also liked him a lot, and didn't want to go to sea because I feared I would miss him. Looking back, boy was that stupid!

As a young person, I had often been lonely, so having a boyfriend was important to me. I was also a little apprehensive about going to sea as an officer and hanging my license "in the rack."[2]

It's one thing to be a midshipman, as no one really expects you to know very much. It's entirely another thing to be responsible for a huge steel vessel that, weighing thousands of tons, takes a mile to stop, and carries hundreds of millions of dollars' worth of cargo. I chickened-out and followed my boyfriend's advice.

I'd decided to look for a shore-side job—and there it was: Shell Oil. It seemed everyone was sending off résumés for this job, so I figured I'd jump in, too. Plus, the job was in Houston, so at least I'd be within a reasonable range of my boyfriend, should I get the job.

This immature, short-sighted, and timid decision to apply for a shore-side job was my first career mistake. I used all the wrong reasons, ignored evidence, and let emotions, rather than logic, guide me. That was dumb.

As I reflect on it now, I realize I was very smart and accomplished for my age, yet still very immature. Intelligence and maturity are unrelated traits. I think that while raising me, my parents also confused intelligence with maturity. It's an easy mistake to make.

I set to work scraping together a résumé. Why any college student is expected to provide a résumé is beyond me. At twenty-one years of age I had been, effectively, enrolled in school my whole life. What exactly was I supposed to have accomplished? But I scraped a résumé together and tried to plump it up as best I could.

Let's see—hmmm. I was midshipman-in-charge of the Merchant Marine Museum on campus; I had good grades; I was a company executive officer for the corps of midshipmen; I'd grown up on boats; I had a black belt in Aikido—but *so what*? What did any of that have to do with Shell Oil? To boot, there was something extraordinary about every one of my classmates, or they wouldn't have been at Kings Point in the first place. I felt like a wagging puppy in a pet store window, next to a dozen other wagging puppies, hoping someone would pick me.

I sent off my application to Shell Oil and decided I'd better attend one of the career seminars the school was offering, just in case I were to land an interview.

The seminar was put on by a bland-looking man wearing a predictably unremarkable suit, who droned on about what to do and not do at interviews. I sat, as arrogant twenty-one-year-olds will do, with my arms folded, unimpressed, as he spoke about professionalism, firm handshakes, eye contact, and all the other stuff I'd heard before. But then he related a particularly useful anecdote.

He told of a man being interviewed by a major computer company. The candidate had been taken out to lunch and had ordered a steak—medium-rare—and a nonalcoholic beverage. So far, so good. But then, as the man chatted casually with the interviewers, he proceeded to salt his food—without having tasted it first.

Allegedly, the employer deemed such behavior an indicator of a personality far too reckless for their conservative firm, and he was not hired.

My interest was piqued. I sat up and listened. The speaker went on to talk about the all-important "interview lunch."

"Don't order anything with a sauce or anything that doesn't match the color of your suit," he said. "Tomato soup is definitely out. Order something that won't show if you dribble it on your chest."

I realized my interview suit—the only one I owned—was the color of oatmeal, which severely limited my dining options.

He went on.

"Order nothing that has to be eaten with your hands. If you order chicken or pizza, eat it with utensils. Don't order a salad like hearts of romaine, because the pieces may be too big to eat neatly. Always leave something on your plate—and not just the vegetables. And absolutely do not order an alcoholic beverage, even if encouraged to do so."

He talked about cologne and perfume and other grooming issues. Then he gave us some pointers on how to answer those pesky questions that have no right answer. Questions such as, "Have you stopped beating your wife?"

We were taught that if an interviewer asked, "So, Mr. Jones, what are your worst traits?" we were to turn it into a positive by answering, "Well, I tend to work too hard and I'm a bit of a perfectionist. Oh, and I probably get too upset when people don't show up on time or don't follow instructions. Those are pet peeves of mine."

After that presentation I was armed and ready for any interview—or so I thought.

I wasn't at all ready when a plebe (a Kings Point term for freshman) knocked at my door to say there was a call for me at the phone bank down the hall. (We didn't have phones in our rooms and cell phones had not yet been invented.) It was Shell Oil. I raced to the phone. A sweet, southern voice informed me I was one of three midshipmen who had been selected to interview for the job, and that I was to be flown to Houston within the month. I was happy, but I was nervous.

The other two candidates were another young woman and a young man. It seemed obvious that Shell wanted a woman. Shell's selection of two female applicants was statistically improbable, since Kings Point had very few women, and many male midshipmen had applied for the job. Also revealing was the fact that the male cadet Shell selected was not the male applicant with the highest grades. Shell obviously wanted a girl. I knew there'd be heat—and there was.

"They're only interested in you because you're a girl!"

"Hey, what's she got that we ain't got—besides two tits?"

"You wouldn't ever have gotten that interview if you weren't a girl."

I knew they were right. I knew that male cadets who had better grades than mine had applied and had not been selected. The taunting became so bad in class one day that I whipped around and attacked back.

"You're probably right. I probably did get the interview because I'm a girl. But I'm qualified—probably better than most of you jerks. And for every break I've gotten because I'm a girl, there have been a hundred setbacks, like having to go to school with you idiots every day. So this is payback time."

What the heck did they expect me to do? Turn Shell down?

One fellow shot back, "You wouldn't even be here if you weren't a girl!" That was a lie. Many of the women cadets had higher grades and scores than the men and were a lot tougher, but facts didn't matter—perceptions did.

I countered, "And you wouldn't be here if your daddy wasn't a rear admiral." That pretty much ended it. They left me alone after that.

It was the spring of 1986. I flew to Houston the day before the interview. Shell put me up in the fanciest hotel I had ever seen, the Houston Sheraton. That night, as I waited restlessly for the clock to tick off the hours until my morning interview, I luxuriated in a bubble bath, and was surprised to find a mint on my pillow at bedtime. I even ordered room service. I laid out my oatmeal-colored suit for the next morning and called my parents to tell them of my good fortune. I could tell how happy they were for me. I was happy too.

The next morning I awoke and showered. I tried to do something with my hair, but it was too short to have many options. Back then, the academy required that women's hair not touch the bottom of their collars. So I fussed with my hair until I got frustrated; then I gave up and just got dressed.

Shell Oil headquarters occupied two city blocks in the center of Houston. Exxon was just up the street, as were many other major oil companies. I reported to Human Resources for the first stage of my interview. Once there, I was issued a security badge and instructed to fill out a stack of papers. I was then escorted to a series of other offices for interviews. One of the interviewers even asked me to describe my worst traits. When I started with my turn-it-into-a-positive answer, the man stopped me with a raised hand and asked, "Career lecture series?" I flushed, smiled, and looked down at my lap.

"Glad to see you made the effort," he offered with a smile.

While being shuttled from floor to floor, escorted by a Human Resources representative at all times, there was a delay. We were waiting in one of the expansive and richly appointed lobbies when I noticed the many oil paintings on the walls. The escort explained that Shell featured different artists each month, which enlivened the lobby with a sort of rotating art show.

"It must be Impressionist month, then," I commented.

I could tell the Human Resources fellow was impressed that a maritime cadet would know something about art. I explained that I had learned a little about art in a required class on Western Civilization. What I didn't tell him was that I had spent most of my Western Civilization class silently pouting, with my mental arms folded, rejecting all the mushy topics (those seemingly irrelevant to my degree) that were being shoved down my throat. I loathed that class—we all did.

What *he* didn't tell *me* was that Shell Oil wanted well-rounded employees—people who, in addition to being competent mariners, were also cultured and house-broken. Shell wanted people who could be groomed into higher management positions. Shell didn't care so much that I was a competent mariner. "Knuckle-dragging deck-apes", as one engineering cadet called us, came a dime-a-dozen. Shell wanted employees who had some worldly knowledge in addition to technical competence.

Finally, we were on the move again. I was taken to the Marine Department, where I was to have the last interview of the day. The head of the Marine Department, I had heard, was an older, Dutch man who used to sail as a tanker captain. I assumed his word would be final, on whether I was ultimately hired or not. All the previous interviews, all with men, were mostly pro forma, to be sure I had the right basic qualifications on paper and was reasonably presentable. The captain's decision, I was sure, was what mattered.

I sat in the captain's office to wait for him. Aside from the normal knickknacks common to most executive offices, photographs of ships and tanker piping diagrams covered his walls. One such diagram hung on the wall next to me at about eye level; I scrutinized it as I waited.

"I wonder if he's going to ask me some tanker question," I mused. I hoped he would, as I knew tanker operations better than any other type of cargo operations.

Finally, the captain entered and shook my hand. He looked to be about sixty, weathered, with twinkling blue eyes peeking out from beneath bushy gray eyebrows. He looked exactly like I expected a sea captain would, sturdy and fit, with big, callused hands, and he had a distinctive Dutch accent. He asked about my tanker experience as a cadet, and asked why I wanted to work for Shell.

That was one question for which I hadn't prepared. For what felt like an eternity, I searched for a clever answer. I recalled vaguely the career advisor mentioning that one should know the history of the company and "show them you do your homework." Funny, doing my homework is exactly what kept me from researching anything about Shell's history. Finally I gave up and stated the obvious.

"I need a job. I love tankers and I have good grades and Shell has a job opening, so I thought I'd apply."

"Gut!" he replied. "How 'bout zum lunch." He had a car brought around from the company pool. I was very impressed. He and I and two other marine guys piled in and set off for lunch.

"Do you like barbecue?" he asked, turning around to look at me. "Because we are going to the best barbecue in Texas. Real authentic."

I quaked. Nothing at a barbecue is the color of oatmeal! Sauce. Beans. Corn. Beer. Can I use a toothpick? And beans! Oh God!

After driving well beyond the city limits, we pulled off the two-lane road and stopped in a cloud of dust, the only sedan in a cluster of pickup trucks. The place certainly looked authentic. It was the only structure around. The menu, a wood board, weathered and gray with faded lettering, was brief. Ribs, brisket, beans, corn on the cob, and beer. So much for hearts of romaine.

I wondered whether it was all a set-up. Realizing I'd been beaten, I threw my fate to the winds and ordered a whole round of everything—even the beans. I didn't order a beer but that was only because I don't like beer. By the end of the meal, I had sauce running down my wrists, corn and pepper stuck in my teeth, and I could feel the beans starting to produce that familiar bloated feeling. I figured I'd best at least enjoy the meal, since I probably would never be back in Texas.

After lunch we went back to the main office, where the old sea captain asked me a few general tanker questions. Then, it was over. I was given a plane ticket back to New York, and told they would be in touch.

A few weeks later, an excited plebe knocked on my door saying Shell was on the line. I didn't believe it. Not that I didn't think I had a chance of landing the job, but it was April Fools' Day, and lots of pranks were being played. The plebes knew that seniors were waiting for job calls, so when a company called for someone, they got excited too. But on April Fools' Day, the plebes were having a little fun with us. I slowly walked down the hall and, picking up the phone while shooting a glare towards the plebe, demanded, "Okay, who is this?"

"This is Mrs. Johannes from Human Resources at Shell Oil in Houston, Texas, and we would like to offer you the marine analyst job. Please let us know your decision within two weeks. We have sent confirmation and a reply form in the mail."

I couldn't believe it—I had my first real job!

2

Improvise—Adapt—Overcome: Quitting My First Job

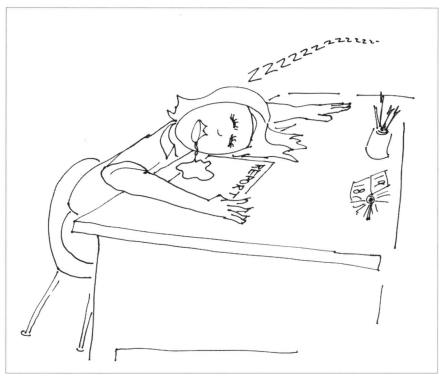

"Bored as a Boy in Church" by Michael J. Durnan

The job started in August. Shell Oil was so helpful with my move that the transition from college wasn't as stressful as I'd anticipated. I had two weeks to find a place to live, while Shell paid the bill for me to stay at the Houston Sheraton. Despite the luxury of the hotel, I was eager to find an apartment, as I'd never had a place of my own. Houston had (as I'm sure is true of other cities) real estate agents who would drive apartment-hunters around the city to visit various complexes. The agents were very capable, so it wasn't long before I found a comfortable second-story apartment that was close to downtown, and my work.

I bought most of my furniture from thrift stores, at rock bottom prices. I fashioned my first bed from a sheet of plywood laid over two waterbed drawers, with an air mattress thrown on top. I splurged on a new couch. I had been given graduation presents of flatware and even a cookbook, so it wasn't long before I was settled in.

Finally, my first day at work arrived. Again sporting my stylish oatmeal suit, I was introduced to everyone in the Marine Department. Each staff member was responsible for a specific geographic region. There was a man assigned to overseas concerns, and one for each coast of the United States. I was to be responsible for the Marine Department's interests in the Gulf of Mexico crude oil system. I was the only woman on the floor who was not a secretary. I was young, new, and a bit uncomfortable.

I was assigned a mentor, and I tagged along with him for the first few months. Though my mentor was available to answer my work-related questions, I was never included in the guys' casual lunches, after-work visits to the local pub, or other social gatherings. I just attended meetings and interacted normally during the work day. The secretaries seemed a little resentful of me, so having lunch with them was out of the question. Usually, I ate lunch alone and proceeded directly home after work.

At the time, I thought nothing of it. I was young, pretty, and female. I understood how awkward it could be for a man—especially a married man—to invite a young woman like me out after work, even if just to join a group of co-workers. I don't think their leaving me out was intentional or consciously discriminatory. Also, on my account back then, I didn't have the courage to pop my head over the cubicle walls like a whack-a-mole carnival game and ask, "Can I join you guys after work?" Nor did I have the graciousness to introduce myself to the secretaries and invite *them* to lunch, rather than waiting for them to invite me.

Looking back, I realize how much I missed by not being included in those informal gatherings. Now I appreciate how much work gets done at off-site and after-hours gatherings. Critical networking often happens at informal meetings after work. Many important decisions are made outside of office hours and off-site.

I made a lot of mistakes at Shell, mostly in what I *didn't* do.

Shell would charter (i.e., rent) most of its marine equipment, such as barges and ships, rather than own them outright. This is not uncommon in the industry, as it helps shield large corporations from some types of legal liabilities.

One of my primary duties was to survey barges and observe crews whose companies were trying to win contracts with Shell, or that already were chartered by Shell. I was taught to thoroughly inspect and survey barges. I traveled all over the Gulf Coast visiting petroleum barges as they lay at various docks. Also, I was to be the first point of contact should any marine issues arise at any of the crude oil facilities within my region. If I couldn't handle it, the problem would move its way up the ladder. I felt comfortable with the surveying duties, but the rest of the job was a bit over my head. I felt too young and inexperienced for the job and was unclear as to exactly what I was to do when I was not in the field surveying equipment.

As the weeks passed, I found myself growing bored, probably because I was unclear about what was expected of me and I was either too embarrassed, too shy, or too arrogant to ask. I also felt lonely. I didn't know a soul in Texas, except for one young man who was the son of a friend of my parents.

Bruce was a fellow Kings Pointer who worked as a marine engineer for Exxon, just up the road. At my mother's urging, I finally called him, and we met for lunch. The guy was brilliant—and delightfully odd.

His attire, though not inappropriate, struck me as slightly unconventional. It was as if he was begrudgingly conforming to the corporate mold, while subtly mocking it. He was of average height and slim build, sporting an Einstein mop and slacks that often revealed his ankles. His eyeglasses made his soft brown eyes appear large and liquid; I immediately took a liking to him. He didn't seem to exude the suppressed, edgy hostility to which I had become accustomed at Kings Point.

He confided in me that he had hated his time at Kings Point. I wondered to myself why, if he was so unhappy, he hadn't just left, but he graduated and went to sea as an engineer. Exxon rotated their officers ashore every so often, and he had just been rotated ashore into Exxon's head office for a year or two. He had also just been accepted into a Ph.D. program at the Massachusetts Institute of Technology, and was waiting to hear whether Exxon would grant him a leave of absence to pursue his doctorate degree. He said he wanted to study robotics so he could be an "Imagineer®" at Disney World.

He owned stock in Disney and would make it a point to attend the annual shareholders' meetings so that he would have an excuse to visit Disneyland. He was my kind of guy!

Bruce and I met for lunch often, usually engaging in heated debates over one abstract idea or another, such as whether computer-generated music is really music at all. I relished the intellectual stimulation of his challenging banter.

Once he invited me out to a water park, but I didn't go. I was self-conscious about my figure in a bathing suit. I couldn't tell whether he liked me or was just being polite because our parents were friends, but I was shy that way, so I said I couldn't go. I guess I must have liked him, or I wouldn't have cared so much about my looks.

Looking back, I wish I had today the shapely figure I had back then. Why we women don't realize our own beauty when we are young is beyond me. I felt I was pretty—just not pretty enough.

My contact with Bruce slowly fizzled, probably because I turned down so many dates. I found myself alone in Houston again. The job was beyond me, and I became frustrated and bored. I needed to change something.

Mercy Wright told me that the marines have a saying: "Improvise—Adapt—Overcome." She related her early experiences as she entered the U.S. Marine Corps:

> I can remember going into the military head first, not really looking where I was diving, especially because I just wanted in and to be able to say, "I am a marine." It was a man's world…one to which I would have to adjust—and quickly.[3]

Like Mercy, to be fulfilled and effective in my new job, I realized I too would have to improvise, adapt, and overcome.

On one particularly daunting assignment working for Shell, I was dispatched to Houma, Louisiana, a town some of my colleagues referred to as the "armpit of the world." I was sent there to ensure that the men working on benzene barges (yes—it was only men, back then) were wearing appropriate respiratory protection. Benzene, like many other petroleum products, is a carcinogen. New figures had been published lowering the acceptable limits for benzene exposure, and I was to pass this along and see that everyone was wearing their respirators and protective gear.

Benzene looks and smells deceptively like diluted honey, but it is really bad stuff. Since the late 1980s, tanker personnel have been required to get regular tests to monitor the accumulation of benzene in their blood.

I arrived at the dock in Houma to find the barge already hooked up and pumping benzene to shore. Despite the stifling heat and humidity, I had to wear my official Shell coveralls and hardhat. After parking in the gravel lot near the dock, I checked in at the dock shack. After signing-in, I ambled down the gangway onto the barge, wearing my respirator and carrying a briefcase stuffed with the latest memos from Shell's head office. I tried to look authoritative yet nonchalant.

The man working the barge was an old fellow by the name of Gus. He looked to be about a hundred years old, but he must have been younger. He flashed a toothless smile, and looked me up and down as I approached. The tugboat hung lazily off the pilings of the dock, and one of the deckhands waved as Gus and I made our way past the roaring pump engines, to the barge house on the aft end of the barge.

"What can I do fer ya? Marshmallow treat?" Gus said, his gnarled hand extending a greasy, blackened baking tray half-filled with sticky marshmallow rice treats. On one corner of the tray, a fly was hopelessly stuck, still clinging to life.

"No thank you," I replied, peeling off my respirator.

His eyes were weepy and red from long days on the bright water, and he was half-deaf from decades of working near the roaring engines that drive the barge pumps. I could tell he wouldn't be especially receptive to the idea of donning a respirator, especially in Gulf Coast heat.

"College kid, eh? We just got surveyed a month ago. What do you need?"

"Well, actually I'm here to inform…" I started to answer, and then realized I'd better do some fast thinking, as this was going to require a creative approach.

"Actually…er…the old survey was lost. So I just need to take another look around," I said. (This was a fib.)

"Okay," he said. "No problem. Lemme know if I can answer any questions." Gus flicked the fly out of the marshmallow goo.

Being young, female, and from the head office, I had anticipated some resistance. I knew that I was barely credible to these seasoned oil workers.

In this job, I found my sex was not so much an issue as were my age and inexperience. I was just too young to be credible. Being female didn't exactly help, either. I had to handle these affairs delicately—or else they would backfire.

I poked around the barge here and there, and jotted down a few meaningless notes. As I turned to leave, I said, "Gus, maybe one last thing…" and I let my voice trail off as though I was changing my mind.

"Yeah?"

"Oh…well…geez, I really shouldn't be saying anything. I could get in a lot of trouble," I said, heading toward the gangway to leave.

"What? Say anything about what?" he asked, trying to catch up with me as I kept walking.

"Well, I guess I can tell you, but you have to absolutely promise not to tell a soul. Can you promise me that? I could lose my job if this got out."

"Yeah, sure. What is it?" he implored. I leaned in close enough to smell the cigarette tar and encrusted dirt that clung to his body, and whispered in his waxy ear.

"You see this respirator?" I whispered, holding it up slightly. "Well, I wear it all the time around benzene. Head office found out that this stuff'll make you sterile!"

"No!" he pulled back in shock. "Really?"

"Sterile?" by Michael J. Durnan

I nodded, doubtful of the reproductive options he felt he still had. Giving him a goodbye click and a wink, I headed back up the gangway.

Of course, I had concocted the whole story. It really must have worked, though, because the next day I came back and not only was Gus wearing a full-face respirator, so were the all the guys on the tugboat. Even the cook wore his when he came outside. I may have overdone that one a bit.

That episode is a classic example of how, in order to be effective, women may have to handle situations differently than men. We just have to figure out ways around resistance to our sex and/or our age. I often found it most effective to mix one part humor, two parts white lies, and a dash of artful maneuvering.

The job at Shell was a good one, but not good for me—my soul was shriveling up. I just wasn't the pantyhose and cubicle type. I needed adventure. I needed to go to sea. Originally I told myself that I'd give Shell a year, and if I wasn't happy, I'd quit. That's precisely what I did. On what was exactly my first anniversary with Shell, I told the old sea captain that I had to move on. He knew I wasn't happy, and wished me well. He was probably glad to see me go—for both our sakes. My parents, on the other hand, were sure I'd completely lost my marbles.

I packed my belongings into a small two-wheeled trailer, loaded my cat into my Camaro, and, with my mother along to help with the driving, drove back to California to look for a ship. For myriad reasons, I don't advise driving across country in August, towing an improperly loaded trailer, while accompanied by one's mother and an insubordinate pussycat—but that's another story.

In August of 1987, I headed back home to the lovely San Francisco Bay Area. I have never loved the cool summertime fog that spills over the Marin headlands as much as I did the day I pulled in to my parents' driveway.

I had been away for almost five years. My parents were living in a house now, something I had never known them to do. We had always lived on sailboats. So I camped on my parents' couch, called the union every day, and literally waited for my ship to come in.

While waiting for a ship, and calling the union every day, I worked odd jobs. One temporary job I had was as an apprentice marine surveyor. The owner of the firm hired me to develop a commercial cargo barge inspection program for his company, in order to expand his business. He also intended to train me as a surveyor for smaller craft. Having had Shell's training, it was a breeze to develop a barge inspection form to suit his needs. After a couple of weeks' work, I generated a form that anyone off the street could follow. My form guided the surveyor around the barge, item by item, specifying what to look for, and it even included pertinent regulations next to the applicable sections. It was, I thought, a masterpiece of simplicity and thoroughness.

Other than that task, the job was exceedingly boring. I had accompanied another surveyor on a few fish boat surveys and between trips the boss had me reading survey reports of other vessels. Most of the files involved small pleasure craft and I was getting as bored as a boy in church. I didn't want to seem arrogant or presumptuous, so I never openly complained. I did grumble just a bit but nothing happened. Eventually, I was so bored I started falling asleep at my desk.

I knew the boss had seen me asleep one day. Once I woke up to find I had drooled all over a sailboat survey report I was supposed to be reading, and I was shocked that the guy didn't fire me on the spot. Boredom, for me, is a particularly miserable sort of torment. I finally resolved that if things didn't pick up in another week, I would quit.

A few days after I made my resolution, a new surveyor was hired. He was a fairly young guy in his mid-forties or so, and he was introduced and shown around the small, crowded office. I looked around the office and vaguely wondered where they planned to put this new guy. All the desks were taken—there was absolutely no room for another.

That afternoon I was politely fired. Not really fired—I was "laid off"—which is a nice way to say "fired."

What a blow to my ego. I couldn't believe that a fish boat surveyor had fired me! After all, I had been trained by Shell Oil, and I thought pretty highly of myself. But frankly it was a relief to be out of that boring office.

I was feeling bruised, but, given the arrogance that comes with brains and youth, even after being fired I still felt rather smug—until I remembered that my now former boss had the inspection forms I had developed. I realized that with those forms, he didn't need me anymore. With my foolproof system, he could hire just about *anyone* to survey barges! I'd been used! My smugness evaporated, and I just felt bruised.

I learned a big lesson, and in an instant, the concept of intellectual property rights came alive to me. My knowledge was valuable, and other people could make money knowing what I knew. I vowed to never again give away hard-earned knowledge or training, any more than I would give away my car.

My father, trying to illustrate the value of knowledge, once told me a story about a man who owned an expensive performance car. One day this man noticed his car was running rough, so he took it to the shop. The mechanic raised the hood and had the owner start the engine. Sure enough, it ran rough. The mechanic stood back, stroked his chin, and looked at the engine without uttering a word. Finally, he nodded and went to his tool chest and retrieved a small wrench. Returning to the car, he leaned in and gave a small nut a quarter turn. The car coughed once and then suddenly it was running smoothly, its 300 horsepower purring like a leopard after a fine meal.

"That's wonderful!" exclaimed the owner. "How much will this cost me?"

"One thousand dollars," replied the mechanic.

"One thousand dollars! Why that's outrageous," bellowed the owner. "All you did was spend five minutes stroking your chin, and then you turned one stupid little nut a quarter turn! How can you justify a thousand dollar charge?"

"Because I knew which nut to turn," replied the mechanic calmly.

I learned the value of knowledge that day. While my ego was dented (probably a long-overdue inevitability), I felt wiser and more mature for the experience.

After two failed attempts to endure jobs in cubicles, I decided I'd better try harder to go to sea. One of the major maritime deck officers' unions, the International Organization of Masters, Mates and Pilots (IOMMP), offered few prospects. Their membership books had been closed for some time.

There was another union: the Marine Engineers' Beneficial Association (MEBA). They had jobs for both engineers and mates, but I didn't know how to gain entry. I needed an "in," a contact, a mentor, and a little luck.

I recalled helping a young female plebe who had been falsely accused of cheating, when I was a senior at Kings Point. In a phone conversation with her father, also a Kings Pointer, I was told if ever I needed a job, to call him. His firm operated surveillance vessels that towed U.S. government listening arrays around the oceans. I called and luckily he remembered me. Two days later I was being processed for a top-secret security clearance and I joined MEBA, the union that manned these surveillance boats.

When I called the union headquarters in New York and explained what was going on, the dispatcher, in a thick Bronx accent, said, "Yah really otta wait for a real job, kid. Those boats don't pay fer shit, yunno what I mean? Overgrown tugboats's what they are, yunno what I mean? If you can wait a few days, or weeks maybe, I think I can get you out on a real ship, yunno what I mean? Whaddya say, eh kid? But it's your call. You want da tugboats I'll give ya da tugboats. Yunno what I mean?"

He said all this rapid-fire, without once inhaling, as only New Yorkers can do.

What a dilemma. I felt like my life had just turned into a game show with unknowns behind every door. Is a scrawny bird in the hand better than a long shot at a fatter bird? I decided to gamble and wait for the "real ship." I enjoyed being with my folks, and the hide-a-bed was not really all that uncomfortable.

Ten days later, the phone rang. It was the union with an offer for a job on what was to be my first real ship. I eagerly accepted the offer without hesitation. I was shipped out to a jet fuel tanker in the South China Sea as an able-bodied seaman (an "AB" is a deckhand position, not an officer).

I was the only woman aboard.

3

Super-Rights:
Why Men Bristle

"Bikini Battle" by Michael J. Durnan

♂♀♂

The U.S. Department of Labor defines a "nontraditional" job as one in which less than 25 percent of the workforce is female. During the 1970s and '80s, many male-dominated occupations began to open up for women. In fact, many jobs which the U.S. Department of Labor classified as nontraditional in 1988 were, by 2008, no longer classified as such.[4]

These industries didn't open to women willingly—they were often pried open. There certainly were extraordinary women in earlier decades who were scientists (Madame Curie), marksmen (Anne Oakley), spies (Mata Hari), and women who did other "manly" things, but they were rarities.

During the second half of the twentieth century, many tough gender battles were fought, landmark sexual harassment and discrimination laws were passed, and lawsuits were won.

I have read and heard stories of women who blazed trails into male-dominated professions. The term "blazed trails" is apt, indeed. For many women the struggle was arduous, and in some cases, dangerous.

I recently read the doctoral dissertation of California Maritime Academy's police chief, Dr. Roseann Richard. As part of her research she interviewed several female law enforcement executives, each of whom held the rank of captain or above. The ordeals many of these women endured in the 1970s and later were horrendous. These police women described potentially life-threatening refusals to provide back-up to them, and intentional interference with their radio communications during police calls.[5] Such behavior seems unthinkable in today's world but many of the laws and policies to protect against such behaviors didn't exist back then.

Sometimes, even what appears to be chivalry can backfire. Chief Richard told me of a male colleague who would try to be chivalrous by opening her police cruiser's door, and doors to buildings to let her enter first. While she appreciated the gesture, the unintended consequence was that she wound up being the primary officer on the calls and as such she got stuck writing the reports!

These courageous police women and all the other women who pierced gender barriers contributed to the freedoms, rights, and equality in the workplace that I have enjoyed for over twenty years.

As a cadet back in the 1980s, I was interested in becoming a navy fighter pilot. I was told that women were not allowed to fly navy combat jets, but they were allowed to fly military cargo planes. Fighters are often used to protect the highly valuable cargo planes, much like naval escorts are sent to protect cargo ships in convoy. Apparently the navy was comfortable letting women fly as a target, but uncomfortable letting women shoot back! I found this baffling, but instead of fighting it, I just picked another job.

Now, women can, and do, fly fighter jets for the navy. My law school class was roughly 50 percent female. Now, there are female Supreme Court Justices, admirals and generals, police chiefs, and snipers. There are fisherwomen and female sea captains. I see women on construction crews and engineering teams. There are women surgeons and race car drivers. I see women working at quickie oil change businesses. And let's not forget the female astronauts, the past and present Secretaries of State, or the first woman elected as Speaker of the House of Representatives.

Even with all the women now in powerful positions, some forms of sex-based harassment and discrimination still exist, and I suspect they always will. The big difference now is that most organizations have policies addressing the subject and laws prohibit truly egregious behavior. But even the best training, laws, and policies can't change people's attitudes and behaviors. Even if there is no overt harassment, there is bound to be some lingering resentment and, at a minimum, some subtle discrimination when women enter a male-dominated workplace.

Based on my experience and observations, I have come to believe that how you handle yourself will determine much of what you experience, but not all. Sometimes things just go terribly wrong, despite one's best behavior.

The Flight or Fight Spectrum

Some women choose to fight for these, and similar opportunities. There is a spectrum of assertiveness, and everyone falls somewhere on it. While some women think it wise or even obligatory to stay and fight for what they think is fair and right, others think it wiser to simply avoid or leave hostile environments. There is a spectrum of attitudes on this subject and I honor each woman's decision to do what she determines is best. Not everyone is cut out to be a trailblazer.

People like Mahatma Gandhi, Dr. Martin Luther King, and Nelson Mandela sacrificed enormously to fight for what they believed was right. The women who went before us sacrificed and fought to earn women the same opportunities as men. You and I, as women in the modern workforce, are the beneficiaries of their struggles.

If workplace conditions get bad, you almost always have a choice. You can stay and fight or you can leave. If you tend toward the "avoid trouble" end of the spectrum, you may choose to transfer to another location, or simply quit. If you are closer to the "fight for what is right" end of the spectrum, you may choose to stay and fight for your rights. There are positions all along the spectrum. All have merit. Where you fall on the spectrum will change with age, experience, and your situation in life. I know that over the years I have changed my position many times. Some things were worth fighting for and some weren't.

Understand, however, sometimes you can be right, and still be miserable.

You have the right, and in most cases, the legal obligation, to report harassment to your superiors, but whenever you do so— despite written policies against retaliation—you may still pay a price.

Quitting has a price. Staying and fighting has a price. Everything you do and every decision you make has a price. The decisions you don't make are themselves decisions—they too exact a price.

If you face sexual harassment or discrimination in the workplace, you will need to decide for yourself whether it is better to stay and fight, or better to move on to a more civilized environment. There is honor and wisdom in either.

Stay as Free as You Can
and Keep Your Options Open

As a young woman, I just wanted to be free, make money, and have adventures, so I was closer to the "avoid confrontation" end of the spectrum. Had a particular ship proved to be a nightmare, I probably would have just quit the ship. In my field, it was easy to quit a ship and catch another one. That was one aspect I loved about the industry. I was completely free and nimble, especially so by working through a union where I was just a license with a number.

I know that some jobs or situations aren't very easy to leave, such as the military. I was fortunate in that I never had a situation spiral so out of control that quitting would have been the only option. I was also prudent in that I never let financial problems or other obligations get so cumbersome that I couldn't have quit if I wanted to. It was critical to my well-being that I be free in every sense of the word.

For me, being happy and fulfilled was more important (some may say selfish) than trying to correct every little wrong. Being happy and fulfilled meant being safe, valued, free to live and work as I pleased, when I pleased, and where I pleased. I never expected anyone to make me feel welcomed. I just expected to be let alone to do my job, and given the same levels of support as everyone else.

Based on fifteen years of counseling college women, I have observed that many deny themselves these freedoms by obligating themselves too deeply, too early. I observe young women's dreams hampered and hear of their frustrations when they commit to relationships, have unplanned/unwanted children, and/or get deeply in debt before they are ready for the stability such conditions demand.

If you want to be free, ensure that you arrange your life responsibly in order to pursue your ultimate goals. Don't commit yourself to an irrevocable commitment and then decide you still have some wild oats to sow—that is irresponsible and unfair to the people to whom you committed, and yourself.

Resentment Is Not Necessarily Harassment

There are many books and articles written about sexual harassment, hostile work environments, and how to handle such situations. All employees will, in the modern workplace, be made aware of laws and policies on harassment, and how to file complaints and address concerns. But, there are not many books written on the abuse of the system by greedy or hyper-sensitive women and the long-term impact on the workplace of groundless claims. After all, if there are both good and bad men, there are both good and bad women.

I want to inject some balance into the discussion by sharing with you some stories of women who, in my opinion, abused their power by claiming harassment or hostile work environments with very little provocation. Abuses of the system, no matter how infrequent or long-ago, generate long-term resentment and may undermine your ability to be taken seriously when dealing with justified claims of harassment. Understanding some of the abuses will help you understand why some men are wary of women in the workplace. Recognize too, this book is aimed at women who live and work closely with men, not women who work in large office buildings or labs, and who go home every night.

At sea, I was still a novelty, but nothing like the first female officers who went before me in the late 1970s. The trail, though still relatively new in the 1980s, had been blazed for me.

As you enter the male-dominated professions, be sure your ultimate goals are clear. Most of us seem to be wired a little differently from the average woman, or we would not have chosen such unusual careers. So, what is so attractive about nontraditional careers? Obviously, the job offers something men want—and we want it, too.

Male-dominated professions usually offer the money, power, adventure, or status we desire. It is my opinion that you should focus on your original goals, the reasons you were attracted to the job in the first place. Don't enter the field looking for a fight, or expecting to bend deeply-rooted traditions overnight. Adaptation and change takes time. The men must adapt to your presence and you must adapt to them. They don't know your history or past experiences and you don't know theirs. They will probably assume the worst, based on their past experiences.

Stereotypes

Stereotypes and assumptions based on gender can and do work both ways.

I was chatting with some girlfriends who said they were comfortable with a male nurse, even a male gynecological nurse, just not in any obstetrical capacity delivering babies. Other girlfriends admitted to thinking there is just something "wrong" with a man who wants to teach second grade or drive a school bus. Obviously, many of us women have our own stereotypical mental cartilage. I am not arguing there are no differences between men and women, nor that stereotypes aren't based in societal norms and statistical truths. I believe they often are. I just want to highlight that women also make assumptions and pigeon-hole people based on gender. When you enter the workplace, everyone there will assume you are some version of women with whom they have previously worked.

Don't Abuse Your Power

As women in a "man's world" we owe a profound debt of gratitude to the women who tamped the rocky path into the non-traditional workplace. Their struggles should be honored with our gracious competence and reasonable expectations of the men and employers with whom we work.

My observations are that some women are anything but gracious and reasonable in the workplace. Some of the women I observe seem either hypersensitive or aggressively coiled, like ill-tempered cobras, waiting to attack and looking for a fight.

I have observed women enter male-dominated workplaces, only to become angry and frustrated when the environment didn't immediately adapt to their presence. Let go of unreasonable expectations. Don't expect people in industry, or the military or law enforcement worlds to perform gymnastics trying to accommodate unreasonable expectations or adapt to your particular sensitivities. It is unreasonable and illogical to simultaneously expect equality and then demand special treatment. Both sides must adapt to each other, and don't forget you are a relative newcomer and not the norm.

Again, we all owe a huge debt to the women who endured real struggles to achieve the rights and legal protections we now enjoy. Let's honor their struggles by neither abusing those rights nor our newly-won power. Here are a couple of examples of abuse of female power that have negatively affected the men involved and shaped their interactions with women in the work-place. These stories help explain some of the resentment you may encounter.

Groundless Claims
of Harassment or Discrimination

I have noticed that some women who complain about girlie calendars and posters in the workplace also read Vogue, Cosmopolitan, or Victoria's Secret in the workplace. They are the same women who themselves wear bikinis or dress provocatively in front of male colleagues, and then get upset when men look at them. To me, this is hypocritical.

The argument can be made that girlie posters are inappropriate and serve to sexualize the workplace. While I agree they may be somewhat immature and inappropriate, in some industries they may have been the norm for decades and expecting them to come down because a female enters the workplace may create more resentment than it's worth. Personally, I was never bothered by a pretty woman on a poster or calendar. (A little jealous, maybe.) Sexually explicit images in common work-spaces, however, would make me uncomfortable and I'd have to decide if it was worth complaining about or not. If there is an image or informal practice that sexualizes the workplace or makes you uncomfortable, you'll have to decide if it's worth doing something about. If you decide it is, you're probably going to be more effective if you don't come on like a sledgehammer. I dare say there are men who are uncomfortable around sexually explicit materials, too. I have

"It Has to Go!" by Philomena "Phil" Sulzen

never felt justified in commenting on what people keep in their personal spaces, even if I happened to glimpse it. Such information may, however, give you insight to a person's character and values, just as bumper stickers do.

In the 1960s, my friend Pat Winter's family owned a car dealership. She grew up hanging around the shop and interacting with the mechanics. She still works in the automotive industry. She told me about what she called "the good old days" at the dealership where pranks and dirty jokes were the norm, and everyone got along. In the 1960s and '70s, it was not unusual for a manager to stash bottle of whiskey and some pornographic magazines in a bottom desk drawer, and nobody cared. Pictures of sexy girls adorned spark-plug calendars, and every mechanic's station displayed some sort of girlie poster.

In the mid-1980s, things started to change. Pat noticed younger women coming to work at the dealership who would intentionally look for some way to claim sexual harassment and then get paid to drop the complaint and leave.

"These girls were not really offended or harassed," relates Pat. "They just wanted something for nothing. They wanted a free ride. They didn't want the so-called 'problem' fixed—they just wanted money."

As a result of several such claims, the jokes stopped, posters and calendars came down, and the entire atmosphere of the dealership changed. The shop floor became chilly and quiet.

"This was happening all across the industry," reported Pat. "Now, car dealerships are sanitized places where men get scared and clam up whenever a new female gets hired. Those lazy, greedy [women] screwed everything up for women like me. They ruined what used to be a fun industry."[6]

Pat relates that many of her male friends think women have ruined the automotive industry by being hypersensitive and easily offended. Pat agrees. She feels her job has been made more difficult as a result of the many frivolous claims brought by women. Obviously, not everyone agrees that the industry is worse off, but there are women who prefer the old "rough and tumble" bawdy workplace better than the gentler, but perhaps chillier, modern environment.

On California Maritime Academy's training ship, I have seen male cadets instructed to remove bikini posters from their private lockers, the theory being such posters are demeaning and offensive to women. Yet, I routinely see female cadets on the upper sunbathing deck, a much more public place than a locker in an all-male berthing area, allowed to wear even skimpier bikinis. The sunbathing deck is one of very few public places on the ship where people can go to relax. In my opinion, this double standard, no doubt born of very good intentions, is hypocritical and unfair. It undermines the argument for equality and highlights the (unintentional) duplicity of many institutions' harassment policies. My institution's tolerance of women wearing sexy bikinis in a public space (but not images of them on the inside of a locker door) has the unintended fallout of rendering the upper deck an uncomfortable place for many of my male colleagues, who refuse to go there because they don't want to be accused of "leering" should their eyes fall on a pretty female cadet in a bikini.

On the training ship, it is customary for cadet divisions to paint murals on the bulkheads and machinery. Usually the artwork is lovely. On the overhead of the shaft alley on our current training ship, some cadets recreated the ceiling of the Sistine Chapel. It is gorgeous.

A few years ago, on our previous training ship, a female cadet complained about some nautical artwork. As a result, a lovely, tasteful, mermaid mural that had been up for years was altered because its nipples showed. One cadet told me they were so upset with the order to erase the "offensive" body parts, they wanted to paint out the entire mural. I couldn't blame them.

The administration, surely feeling itself in a bit of a pickle, capitulated to the complaining woman. The appeasement of one woman came at a heavy cost to morale and it planted a seed of distrust in many male cadets. There were many women aboard (I was one) who were saddened to see the mermaid altered. The seed of distrust still exists in the minds of many of the male cadets from that cruise who are now in the work force.

Women must understand that, regardless of how reasonable or fair they themselves may be, they will be working with men who have experienced or witnessed some sort of unfairness or abuse of female power.

Super-Rights

The unintended fallout of the new laws awarding women "super-rights,"—rights above and beyond the rights of men—is that men often shy away from females in the workplace. Whether it's true or not, some men view a woman in a nontraditional workplace as a menacing porcupine who could ruin a career with a simple complaint. Not all men feel this way, but given their past experiences many do. Unfortunately, having one bad experience in the workplace can offset years of smooth, collaborative interactions with women.

Some women fostered this chilly environment by demanding not just equal rights, but super-rights. I personally never wanted super-special rights, just equal rights. But that is no longer the legal state of affairs.

Women and racial minorities, just to name a few, are now protected classes. Did you know that some crimes motivated by racial hatred, for example, carry stiffer penalties than do the exact same crimes perpetrated for purely monetary reasons?

Being the purported beneficiary of such laws, I believe that by making people more unequal, such laws only breed resentment. Whether or not you agree with the fairness of such laws, they have created differing levels of legal protections and rights based on one's genitalia, melanin, sexual orientation, age, and other involuntary factors—and some (perhaps many) people resent this.

According to many men I have spoken to, a woman's presence in a nontraditional workplace, through no fault of her own, will often increase stress for many of her male co-workers due to the imbalance of legal protections.

Be sensitive to their perspective. I have found the "protected class" status to be nothing but a barrier between me and my male colleagues. I want equal rights, not super-rights. Super-rights have spoiled everything.

Once you've established yourself as a reasonable person, one who is willing to make reasonable adaptations and who doesn't expect an entire industry to change overnight, the tension will ease and social interactions will normalize. Don't fault the guys for tiptoeing around you at first. By your relaxed attitude, humor, and competence, they will realize you are just there to work. They will relax and embrace you into the fold.

Bring on the Stress!

With the best of intentions, one of the disservices today's educational facilities inflict on protected classes is to create layers of protections from real-world challenges—the same real world for which the institutions are supposedly preparing them. Our schools are creating politically correct safe havens and "safe learning environments" that are nothing like the real world.

I don't oppose civility and control in the classroom—quite the contrary. Interestingly, however, a recent California State University code requiring civility was struck down by the courts as an unconstitutional restriction of Constitutionally protected free speech rights.[7] I am advocating exposure to the emotional rigors of the real world, especially in the training of people entering "mission critical" disciplines.

Mission critical disciplines are those jobs where bad decisions have devastating impacts on lives, the environment, and/or the economy. Mission critical disciplines include occupations such as the military, law enforcement, firefighting, air traffic control, emergency room doctors, astronauts, and ship's officers. Spreading the net wider, one could even include other transportation-related positions, such as train engineers (consider the lives lost and the environmental damage when trains collide) and bus drivers. In such disciplines, decisions often have to be made quickly, by one person, usually under stress, and with incomplete information.

One could argue that astronauts and doctors are not really mission critical positions, as the effects of a bad decision in space or in an operating room would impact relatively few lives and probably not severely impact the environment. Their mistakes could, however, be very costly.

In contrast, a poor decision by a ship's officer could impact hundreds of lives, destroy the environment, and impact local economies at a scale far beyond the average airplane crash or train collision. Just consider the environmental devasta-

"Chocolate Pudding" by Michael J. Durnan

tion and fiscal impact of a major oil spill, such as the 1989 grounding of the tanker *Exxon Valdez* in Alaska's pristine Prince William Sound.

I am concerned that upon graduation, students who have been over-protected from emotional stresses are at a distinct disadvantage. Over-protection leaves students under-prepared for the psychological stresses of unforgiving industries. Preparation for the real world is the best long term protection. In fact, many of us have seen the results of over-protection.

A few years ago, a male faculty member at California Maritime Academy was unofficially scolded by the administration for "making" a female cadet cry during a simulation training exercise. Actually, the instructor had done nothing different to this student. It was the stress of the simulation scenario to which she had reacted. She was passed through the simulation class, finished the required curriculum, and graduated.

Scuttlebutt has it that during her first bridge watch aboard a crude oil tanker, she froze when a give-way vessel failed to give way. Before the captain had even arrived on the bridge, the young officer was in tears. She was let go at the next port, not for having failed to handle the traffic situation—an advanced situation for a new third mate—but for having broken down with such minimal provocation.

It is my opinion that the institution's leadership and academic programs shortchanged her. By failing to stress her appropriately, we failed to prepare her for the inevitable stresses of the industry—but stressing students is not acceptable in today's academic pedagogy.

As a freshman at Kings Point in the 1980s, I was confused by all the yelling and name calling, all the ridiculous physical requirements, such as running to every class inches from the curb, and the requirements to memorize menus and endless trivial tidbits about the academy. I couldn't understand why they would harass us so much after they had just selected us—the fortunate few—from thousands of applicants. If they didn't want us there, why did they invite us?

It was several years after graduation, when I correctly remembered and followed a series of verbal instructions, told me at rapid-fire pace in a stressful and dangerous situation, when I finally understood.

I had been yelled at by the best of them. I had been forced to memorize and respond correctly under stress. As a cadet, I had been stressed physically, mentally, and emotionally. I realized that situations might arise that I couldn't handle due to lack of experience or expertise, but I knew that nothing would make me cry, freeze, vapor-lock, or otherwise break down. For this, I was grateful.

The best thing we can do for young women—indeed, for every candidate entering mission critical positions—is to train them to be completely technically competent, as well as emotionally robust. We should arm them with some clever tactics for defusing socially, sexually, or racially charged situations.

Imagine if, in the training of airline pilots, emergency room doctors, police officers, firefighters, or even circus performers, all psychological and social stressors were removed and no one could call them bad names, scare them, startle them, or make them feel uncomfortable in any way. Would those coddled candidates be the best prepared? I dare say they would not.

Instead of protecting the protected classes, I argue we should prepare them. Rather than shielding students with speech codes, we should arm them with competence, humor, thick skins, and the desensitization necessary to perform well, even under the inevitable stresses of their profession. This conditioning, though probably emotionally uncomfortable at first, cultivates actual competence and thus, well-placed confidence.

Training for mission critical disciplines should be tougher than the real thing—not easier, as many institutions have made it. We should create a training environment that prepares young women for the realities of the workplace—especially so if it is a nontraditional workplace. They must be prepared so they won't get rattled, or break down in tears, or think they're going to curl up and die if someone calls them a bad name, shuns them, insults them, or flirts with them.

Students in any mission critical service deserve to be stressed early and often, to strengthen them and desensitize them for worst-case scenarios—which most will never experience. It is my belief that in our efforts to protect the "protected classes," we are inadvertently hindering their development into emotionally strong, unflappable professionals. They deserve better.

Most important, we should stop encouraging and facilitating the assumption of "victim" status. Institutional presentations and training sessions that seem to assume women will be victims can imbue women with a sense of dread, making them fear they will always be fighting an uphill battle because of their sex. While some instances will of course still occur, expecting discrimination and harassment at every turn is just no longer justified.

4

Kit and Caboodle:
What to Take

"Hazmat Bra" by Stephen C. Coutts

ost ships and remote job sites will have some sort of little store selling sundries, or will allow access into town for basic shopping. Depending on the size, location and traditional manning of the facility or vessel, it may or may not have items specifically for women, such as feminine hygiene items, lotions, shampoos, etc. Even the most rudimentary slop chests aboard ships always carry candy, cigarettes, a few basic toiletries (manly staples such as Irish Spring™, Aqua Velva™ and Old Spice™ are almost always available) and a smattering of gloves, boots, socks, goggles and other clothing items (usually not in your size). Military bases are usually much better supplied. Plan on bringing what you need with you.

Luggage

When traveling and working overseas, I advise carrying soft luggage that can be rolled up and won't take up a lot of room in a locker. One piece of luggage I always take as a carry-on is a small athletic duffel bag, which I then use as my ditch bag during "abandon ship" drills. A ditch bag is a good idea for all mariners, soldiers, oil rig workers, and workers in any position where they may have to exit a place in a hurry. In it, I always pack long-sleeved coveralls, a knife, a bright flashlight, sunscreen, important documents, some travel-size female toiletries, and medications. If you get in the habit of taking it with you to every drill, it will be automatic if ever you really do have to evacuate in a hurry.

Every time you fly, pack important documents and medicines in your carry-on bag. Also, be sure to carry at least two pairs of clean underwear, socks, a toothbrush and toothpaste, deodorant, and travel sizes of shampoos and other toiletries in your carry-on—enough to last at least three days. I can't tell you how many times my luggage has been lost on overseas flights. And no, they won't delay a mission or the ship's sailing to wait for your luggage to show up. Once my ship sailed before my luggage had been found and my bags showed up at the next port several days later. All my work clothes and everything I needed, was in that luggage. Be as prepared as you can be to live without your checked bags.

If you plan on buying gifts and souvenirs when you travel, consider packing an extra, empty piece of luggage for all the stuff you'll buy overseas. While in Korea on one of my first ships, and after I'd made some real money, I treated myself to a silver fox fur coat. The darned thing just wouldn't fit in my sea bag, and I ended up lugging it along as a carry-on. What a hassle.

Take a very secure bag you can sling over a shoulder for going to town. Some people like fanny packs, but I preferred a large beach bag with a zippered top. I could put my purchases inside and zip it closed. I also wore a concealed necklace pouch to carry my shore pass, or a copy of my passport, and money. For adventures in town, I also recommend a coin purse to use only for foreign currency. Mixing foreign coins with U.S. coins creates a huge mess. A busy foreign marketplace is the last place you want to be fumbling with your money.

Laundry

Do not take any laundry soap with you. The facility or vessel will either provide the soap that is compatible with the sanitation system or will have it available for sale. Bleach also may be prohibited, if it will interfere with the system's biological waste treatment system.

Regarding communal laundry machines, one thing that makes guys uncomfortable is extricating your lacey unmentionables from the washer or dryer. While they may transfer another man's wet laundry to the dryer, they're likely to leave yours in the washer. I have had male colleagues hold up the entire laundry line by leaving a pile of dirty clothes next to the washer, rather than transfer my clean, wet clothes to the dryer so they could wash their clothes.

This reluctance isn't because the fellows don't like you. They are probably concerned (even sub-consciously) that you—or worse, another man—will walk in on them at precisely the wrong moment, and assume they were enjoying handling your undergarments. To most guys, a female co-worker's panties are as toxic as nuclear waste.

When she was fourteen, our daughter, unbeknownst to us— she knew we would disapprove—had secretly acquired a pair of thong underwear. (Why they're called "a pair" of thong underwear is a mystery to me. There's barely enough thread in them to floss my teeth, let alone be a "pair" of something.) Anyway, she would have gotten away with it, but while she was doing her laundry on the sly, the thong got wrapped around the washing machine agitator and almost burned up the motor. Needless to say, her father was not pleased. I can honestly say I have never seen my rugged, six-foot tall husband as visibly uncomfortable as when he had to unwind his daughter's tiny thong out of the machine.

While he worked as a staff captain aboard a cruise ship, a colleague of mine had to investigate the repeated theft of fancy women's underwear from the crew's laundry. It turned out that some of the crewmen were stealing the expensive garments to give to their girlfriends. In close quarters, even laundry can foment drama.

Take a laundry bag to shuttle your stuff from your room to the laundry. Pillow cases are too small. On tankers, I brought two bags—one for relatively clean clothes and one for toxic work clothes. Don't wash dirty work clothes with your underwear—your more sensitive parts will regret it.

I used to pack black panties to wear specifically during my menstrual cycle. I knew that seeing a woman co-worker's underwear was disconcerting enough for most men, but seeing underwear with a blood spot just might have put them into a coma. I spared them the embarrassment and wore black undies a few days a month, just in case.

Usually, men are uncomfortable around women's underclothes and won't steal them. I suggest you buy a net laundry bag in which to wash all your underwear and bras. Supposedly, it is better for the clothes, but more importantly, it spares your co-workers embarrassment. Even then, don't be surprised if you see a guy in a hazmat suit shifting your laundry to the dryer with tongs.

Feminine Hygiene Items and Toilet Paper

Many remote facilities and ships don't carry feminine sanitary items or menstrual medicines. Take your own. Never, ever flush tampons or sanitary napkins down a system that is not designed to handle them. Many foreign plumbing installations are not nearly as accommodating as those in the States. Since you're probably the only female around, it's not as if you could blame the inevitable clog on someone else. The only thing that should go down the toilet is toilet paper and stuff you have eaten first.

On the subject of toilet paper, in foreign countries, if it is provided at all, toilet paper is made of waxed paper and is the size of a postage stamp. (You know this is true if you have ever traveled.) I always carry a compact packet of tissues in my shore bag, as well as some sani-wipes and gel disinfectant for my hands. Travelers are also well advised to carry a small towel or bandana to use as a hand towel because paper towels are not always available in public restrooms. It can also be used to cover a dirty bench or ledge before sitting down.

As far as hormonal moodiness, some women have no hormonal mood changes at all, while others turn into Tasmanian devils. Know which you are, and be aware of the fact that you may be overly sensitive or emotional due to hormone changes. Don't take it out on your co-workers. I have never found that being lonely and overseas eased my menstrual symptoms.

If you want to really make a guy squirm, leave your feminine products in plain sight. I used this all-natural male repellant to advantage and hid my money and passport in a tampon box. It worked so well, even surly Customs agents wouldn't probe there!

You may have someone assigned to clean your room and make your bed. Even if not, I always stow my feminine necessities well out of view, as you never know who may need to be in your space. Be sure to wrap used feminine items very, very well before placing them in the trash. No one, including a female room-mate, wants to see your menstrual refuse in the trash. Help make everyone comfortable by disguising it. These small courtesies should be maintained at home as well. I know that some of you may balk and argue that menstruation is a natural function, so it shouldn't have to be hidden. Well, so is defecating, and no one wants to see that either.

Soap and Lotions

"A Good Shower" by Stephen C. Coutts

In my experience, glycerin and castile soaps don't leave as much of a soap scum as the fatty, opaque soaps do. Castile soap, in my experience, will rinse off more thoroughly, leaving the shower cleaner. I used to pack my own soaps.

Be careful about buying toiletries in a foreign country if you can't really understand the labels. I was shopping in a Japanese department store once, and, not knowing the right word, I mimed vigorous hair-washing motions to a clerk. Once she understood I was looking for shampoo, her face lit up and she led me straight to the appropriate aisle. I selected a bottle based on its clean, refreshing scent. After using up the bottle, I threw the empty in my trash. The fellow who cleaned my cabin had been doing a poor job of it, and hadn't been making my bed. He spoke a little Japanese, as his wife hailed from Tokyo. He asked me if I had rid myself of my head lice, because he was uncomfortable making my bed if I was still infested. When I asked what made him think I had head lice, he pointed to the empty bottle in my trash. Lesson learned. And I thought I was just buying plain old shampoo!

There is a nifty product available now called Gloves in a Bottle®. I recommend it for working with chemicals, oils, or paints. It goes on like a lotion, but dries to form a protective barrier coat on the skin and makes clean-up a snap.

Take sunscreen. One of the areas I neglected, and am paying for now, was my décolletage. Slather the stuff there or you'll develop a permanent v-neck farmer tan, like mine.

Supplements

If you take vitamins or supplements, pack enough to last for your entire stay. If you're aboard ship, or on an oil rig or at another remote facility, your water will most likely be distilled. This water has no trace minerals and is, so I'm told, not as effective as tap water for hydrating your tissues. In these settings, be doubly sure to take vitamin and mineral supplements with you, and try to eat healthful, balanced meals.

Prescriptions

Don't expect to be able to get prescription medications refilled overseas. Take plenty with you. This includes eyeglasses and

"Phone" by Michael J. Durnan

contact lenses. If you have special medical needs or allergies, you must inform your employer. Also, I wouldn't relish the idea of visiting a foreign doctor for a "female" problem. With the different diet, and the heat, sweat, and dirt you'll be encountering and stress you'll be enduring, yeast infections are not uncommon, and are doubly miserable overseas. I suggest packing over-the-counter remedies for yeast infections, just in case. The last thing I wanted was to be forced to describe my symptoms over the radio or satellite phone in front of a bunch of guys.

"Don't Leave Home Without It®"

It is a prudent sailor's credo to always have a way to get home from any port. If you will be in a foreign country, this advice is sound no matter who you work for. For the military person, this is less of an issue.

"Don't Leave Home Without It®" was the American Express credit card jingle, years ago. By carrying a major credit card, I always had the means to pay my way home. This is "mad money" on steroids. (For you youngsters, mad money is money a woman would keep tucked away, pinned to her bra or tucked in a shoe, to spend on cab fare home, should a date go bad.) For me this meant a passport, my merchant mariner's documents, some cash, and, most important, a major credit card.

If you carry a credit card when you travel, be sure to call the credit card company before you leave and tell them the countries you'll be visiting, so that their fraud department won't freeze the card when they spot unusual purchases being made from overseas. I also keep a photocopy of the front and back of every card I carry, as well as contact information for the three major credit bureaus in case a card gets lost or stolen.

Some captains ask merchant sailors to give them their passports for safekeeping in the ship's safe. I never surrendered my passport. If you're asked to surrender your passport, you'll have to decide for yourself how to handle that situation. Keep a copy of your passport with you whenever you go ashore. Keep a copy in a safe place with your other valuables, both at your new quarters and at home.

Phone Cards and Cell Phones

I carry a rechargeable, prepaid international calling card loaded with plenty of minutes, and all important numbers on an index card. I also keep photocopies of everything with my other important documents. I carry the contact information for the Embassies and Consulates of every foreign country I anticipate visiting.

Be careful with cell phones. Know the rates for roaming, connecting, texting, and the call itself. When near a border, a cell phone may pick up and use a cell tower (and system) of the neighboring country, because that tower is closer. This could result in astronomical roaming rates. Cell phone bills can get expensive quickly. I'm sure you can imagine just how I learned this. (It wasn't pretty.)

Be sure to have the contact information for the person you are supposed to call if you need help. For mariners, this is usually the ship's agent. Often, the local contact person or agency designated by your employer is more trustworthy than local law enforcement.

Be sure you understand your status in the host country. Determine whether you are there as part of a military presence or there working under rights granted by a visa or work permit. Your status will dictate some of your rights and responsibilities ashore. Merchant mariners, having no entry visas, must work through their ship's agents to be reunited with the vessel, should they miss their ship. Merchant mariners overseas are not tourists and are not free to roam the countryside.

You never know what might happen to cause you to need to get home in a hurry. Be prepared.

Your Professional Credentials and Documents

Be sure you have all the documents you need in order to report to your work station or sign on to your ship. As these documents are at least as important as your laptop and cell phone, these should be carry-on items. Be sure to have copies of everything, both at home and in separate carry-on bags. I don't advise keeping copies of important documents in checked luggage, as I've had my bags rifled through numerous times. Some folks even get an international driver license (the American Automobile Association (AAA) issues them) so they can rent cars overseas more easily. I had one, but never did use it. From what I've experienced, foreign rental car agencies are far more interested in your credit card than in any driver license. I don't recommend driving overseas, anyway. If you think the taxis are scary overseas, try driving yourself!

Legal Issues

When deciding what to take with you, even what to buy overseas and take back to the work site and/or living quarters, understand that the commanding officer or boss has control over what can and cannot be brought aboard the vessel or onto the base or work site.

The master of a ship or military supervisor usually does not need probable cause to search any part of his vessel or base. You may have little to no legal right to privacy, and often, the Constitutional protection against "unreasonable searches and seizures" that we enjoy in the U.S. does not apply. Companies operating both overseas and domestically may claim specific rights in their employment and housing contracts. Be sure you understand what is allowed and what isn't.

Many employers now prohibit alcohol in the work place even if national regulations do not. Obviously, illegal drugs are prohibited. If you are taking a prescription narcotic or other controlled substance, you must inform the appropriate supervisor. On military and merchant vessels, the commanding officer has almost complete control over your activities and purchases, both aboard and ashore.

Be aware that some items that may be legal overseas, such as ivory, whale teeth, tortoise shells, and certain other animal parts, furs and skins, and over-the-counter drugs, are illegal to bring into the United States, and certain other foreign countries. Don't take these things aboard a ship, as you could jeopardize the entire vessel. Don't take anything you wouldn't want others to know about, and definitely don't take anything illegal. There is virtually no privacy in any environment where people live and work in close proximity.

5

The Initial Chill:
What to Expect at First

"Lonely In a Crowded Lounge" by Michael J. Durnan

When you first enter a nontraditional workplace, don't expect a warm reception. People, justifiably or not, will be wary of you. Everyone is a product of their past experiences, and you have no idea what your male colleagues' past experiences have been. I think it is safe to say that many men consider themselves as having been wronged by women at some point in their lives, either in the workplace or at home—or both. Some, just as potently, have male friends who have also had bad experiences with aggressive women. The problem is, as I have said before, our culture often protects aggressive women and tolerates behavior from women that society would not tolerate from men.

Understand that your mere presence changes everything for them. The jokes have to stop; girlie calendars come down; the entire climate shifts with your arrival.

As a new officer aboard ship, I usually found it would be *days* before men would feel comfortable enough to tell an off-color joke around me. It was obvious that my mere presence altered their work space. They were wary of me. Not because of any action of mine—I enjoy a good joke as much as the next person—but due to a few hypersensitive yet socially aggressive women who went before me. That type of woman actually made my job harder. The fellows had been conditioned by bad experiences, and knew that the entire weight of their employer, union, or service would come down on them should they offend me—even accidentally.

The Social Balance Is Skewed

As a cadet, I noticed that if I were to sit down on the couch in the officer's lounge to watch a movie, no one would come join me. This would happen even if several guys had said they wanted to watch the movie. Then I noticed that if a man were to sit down first, and I came in later and sat either at the opposite end of the couch, or in a separate chair, that was okay. I realized an important thing I could do for the atmosphere aboard ship was to make people as comfortable with my presence as possible. I learned to never be the first to sit in the lounge or wardroom. I'd let the guys filter in, and then I'd join them. That put everyone at ease.

If these accommodations sound extreme to you, put yourself in a man's place. Usually the men you'll be working with are married or in relationships. They won't want to risk appearing forward, as though they have a special relationship or friendship with you, by sitting next to you. As a result, you may feel you're being shunned, especially at first. Don't take offense—it's not personal. The men are trying to protect their relationships with their wives, as well as with each other.

In addition to not wanting to appear forward, men are afraid of being accused of sexual harassment. For decades now, women have been allowed (some say even encouraged) to accuse men of making "offensive" comments, but women face no repercussions when their charges are proven false. Men have been forced into sensitivity training (even lawsuits) because of accusations from aggressive women who allegedly took offense at an overheard joke, or a poster, or some other supposedly egregious display. No wonder a man may be uncomfortable sitting next to you to watch a movie. What if the movie has a rape scene, or a racially charged situation, or a crude sexual joke? What if he laughs and you don't?

Training Rarely Reflects Real Life

A proper discussion of what to expect in any male-domi-nated profession rightly includes discussing your training and conditioning. Your career starts the instant you set foot in the training facility, academy, or boot camp. If you're lucky like me, most bad things will happen—if they happen at all—during your training. It's hard to say whether my training led me to behave in a way that ensured fewer bad things happened to me on the job, or whether my training was so uncomfortable that the conditions of my employment seemed mild by comparison.

When I was a cadet in the 1980s, no one told us what to expect, except that it would be bad—especially for girls. As cadets we were shipped out for six months at a time, in both our sophomore and junior years. We were given a secret code word to say on a telephone that would alert the Academy that we needed to be removed from the vessel immediately. I was concerned before I ever set foot on a deck. A secret code word? It must be awful out there!

For the most part, what I experienced at sea was just the opposite. Quite often the fellows were tripping over themselves to help me open a heavy tank top, show me how to take bearings, and the like. There was, predictably, the usual percentage of jerks, but nothing horribly disruptive. Actually the proportion of jerks aboard the ships was lower than at school!

When working in a nontraditional field, expect some off-color jokes, some girlie calendars or posters, maybe some pornography, some foul language, some not-so-sensitive comments, and some testing early on. None of those should cause you any lasting harm, nor will you curl up and die if you see a poster of a pretty woman in a bikini. Don't expect to be tortured, teased, or hampered in any way. I wasn't. Often quite the opposite.

You'll be tested not just because you're a girl, but because you're new, and young, and you don't know anything yet. Before the men will relax around you, they need to find out where you stand—and whether you are friend or foe.

Once the fellows see that you are competent and normal and not hypersensitive, you'll fit right in and have an extraordinary experience. If, on the other hand, you expect to be offended and think all men are pigs, I suspect you'll be proven right. That was never my expectation or my experience. I found most fellows to be civil, helpful, bright, and fun to be around. You probably will, too.

As I have said, some of the worst harassment I experienced was during college—not at work. Despite the majority of nice, normal guys at school, I quickly realized there were a lot of jerks at school and that I would have to learn to out-maneuver them verbally. Punching them in the nose was, sadly, forbidden. Some of these jerks managed, either through practice or sub-standard biology, to maintain their "jerk" status well into adulthood, but they were never the majority.

When I first entered Kings Point, it was thought best to keep female cadets geographically clumped, so we were only in the even-numbered companies. There were six "normal" companies of cadets and the seventh was for the band. One year, word came down from Washington that all companies were to be integrated. The female cadets were then split up across all seven companies. I was transferred into Third Company, which housed most of the school's football players. They did not welcome me. Then, to compound matters, I was made the executive officer (XO) of Third Company. As XO, I was in charge of the plebes (freshmen). This appointment only made matters worse.

Some weekends, a few of the male cadets would come back drunk and a little boisterous, and they would barge into my room at all hours of the night and try, half-heartedly, to get in my rack. I never complained because, in those days, I didn't think it would do anything but exacerbate the situation. I was strong enough to shove these big oafs out of my room, and they were usually too drunk to do much other than grunt some curses at me. It was more disruptive than anything else.

We were not allowed to lock our doors without requesting and then posting a special privilege pass to do so. It wasn't like I could lock the door without drawing even more attention to myself. That just wasn't worth it. The worst of it came late one winter night, when several guys came in from a night out and poured some ammonia under my door. Our cleaning supplies came mostly from industrial and government sources. This ammonia was so strong it was supposed to be diluted with water before use. The ammonia seeped under my door and vaporized. I awoke to a choking sensation, as my throat and eyes burned. I was so disoriented, I threw open my window and tumbled out into a snow bank, while wearing only my nightgown. Thank goodness I had a first floor room.

That rattled me quite a bit. I don't recall whether I complained to anyone afterward or not, but I think some of the other male cadets took care of whoever it was who foisted that "prank" on me. Anyway, the harassment stopped after that. That episode was the worst experience I had as a cadet.

I am sure times are far better now, as Kings Point has female faculty in uniform, and there are so many more women at sea now, that it's not such a big deal. The country too, has matured overall.

Women occupy many positions of power that were not open to the fairer sex in the 1980s. The cover of the first 2010 issue of *The Economist* magazine shows an image of Rosie the Riveter flexing her muscles and a byline that reads: "What happens when women are over half the workforce." The story leader reports that within 2010, women will make up the majority of the American workforce.

It reports that, "Women already make up the majority of university graduates in the OECD countries and the majority of professional workers in several rich countries, including the United States." It goes on to predict that, "by 2011 there will be 2.6m more female than male university students in America."[8]

This is a vastly different environment than our mothers experienced, or than I experienced in the 1980s. When I shipped out as a cadet for my sea training, women were quite an anomaly on ships. They still are, though less so.

As a cadet on a ship circumnavigating South America, I worked for a captain who ordered me to do all manner of menial tasks. I was never clear whether it was that he didn't like women at sea or didn't like Kings Pointers. Probably both.

One assignment was to seal the lockers in each of the lifeboats with duct tape. We were transiting the Straits of Magellan at the time. The air was so cold that each breath felt like I was inhaling razor blades. As a result of the cold, there was condensation on the lifeboat fiberglass. No matter how much I rubbed and cleaned, the tape simply wouldn't stick. When I informed the captain of this, he retorted that he had "never had a male cadet complain about the cold!" Perhaps I hadn't phrased it right.

Needless to say, despite earning high grades on my sea project, I didn't get a glowing recommendation from that captain. But

I survived. Later I'll share more of the adventures and mishaps I had. As I grew more confident and capable, my good reputation spread, and I was able to handle most situations with increased humor and ease.

Sometimes, a less-than-hospitable welcome stems from cultural differences. This is especially true overseas or with people from different cultures and backgrounds. I learned this rather soundly when, early in my career, I had to fly to Singapore to catch a ship.

In the 1980s, most American airports were visually indistinguishable from my image of insane asylums. They were painted with the same drab colors—washed-out shades of dinner-mint green, burnt orange, and mushroom. Plastic chairs. Gray food. Endless loops of soothing, wordless music piped to every nook and cranny, even into the bathrooms—just to keep travelers from going berserk, I guess. As I waited in just such an airport, I kept expecting to hear the speaker softly coo, "medication time."

The plastic furniture at this particular American airport was purely functional. Most chairs had someone's initials carved into them, or, if they were padded pieces, the faint smell of urine. Eddies of strange, tired, bored people milled about, clinging to jackets and bags, speaking in undecipherable tongues. The only distinguishing feature was the occasional food counter where one could buy dreadful food at exorbitant prices—food that had to be eaten while sitting awkwardly perched on the edge of an airport row-seat. Traveling to meet a ship was never the fun part of my job.

Cultural Differences

When most people think of Singapore, they swoon with visions of brightly draped Asian beauties and exotic, sexually suggestive flowers. But when *I* think of Singapore, I think of being stuffed into a 55-gallon drum, bouncing in the bed of a pickup truck, being smuggled to my ship like a stowaway. Let me explain, because it didn't start out that way.

The flight to Singapore seemed interminable, as most transoceanic flights do. I landed jet-lagged and stiff. The Singapore airport, however, was another world—nothing like American airports.

"Drum Girl" by Michael J. Durnan

It was paradise—a sea of color and light and cleanliness. It even smelled good. People from every corner of the globe were swirling about, laughing, and dining at fancy restaurants—restaurants with real chairs, and real menus, and glass glasses. Elegant ladies hooked their expensive, sumptuous coats over leather chair backs. The airport was like a swank shopping mall with dozens of ritzy stores glittering and beckoning amidst the bustle.

After I made my way past the shopping area toward baggage claim, I was struck by the most noteworthy feature of the Singapore airport: the amnesty box.

Between the shopping area and baggage claim, at the base of a series of wide, shallow steps, was a vast breezeway, a sparsely featured walkway about fifty feet wide. Everyone had to pass through this walkway to reach any part of the airport. It is the only way in or out. Although brightly lit and heavily monitored, there were no stores, no eateries, no seats, and no advertisements in this area. About thirty feet from the foot of the steps, exactly in the middle of the walkway, was what looked like a large stainless steel mail box, similar to the sort found on any American street corner. The area around the box was featureless. No one was near me, but as I approached I could feel the subtle pressure of eyes on me, as cameras silently followed my every step. On an overhead beam, directly above the box, was a huge sign written in many different languages that warned, "The penalty for drug possession in Singapore is death."

I casually wondered how Singapore defined the term "drug." I imagined what it would feel like to be carrying drugs, to read that sign, and then to decide it would be in one's best interest to make a "contribution" to the box.

Having nothing to donate, I continued past the amnesty box and headed to baggage claim, where I saw a frail, perky Asian man in his fifties holding a sign with my name on it. He was my ship's agent.

Ship's agents are hired to arrange for fuel, provisions, and other supplies, or repairs and services such as garbage pickup for vessels calling at their ports. They facilitate customs and immigration paperwork, make local medical appointments for crew, and deliver crew between the airport and the ship.

Under international agreements, commercial mariners travel without any visas. When we land in a foreign port, the ship's agent takes legal custody of us and delivers us directly to the vessel.

It being the 1980s, the agent was surprised to see that I was female, but I was used to that by then, as there were few female ship's officers in those days.

A niftier aspect of the 1980s was the way ship's officers were treated by some of the shipping companies. Many companies flew officers first-class, and if we needed to stay in a hotel for a layover or to wait for a ship, they were usually very nice hotels. Those days are over now, but for a while, the lifestyle was pretty luxuriant.

As we awaited my baggage, the agent informed me that my ship had been delayed by a storm, so I would have to wait a day or so before it reached port. We collected my sea bag and headed to his car. He drove me to the hotel where I would be put up, under his recognizance, until the ship arrived.

The stunning teak and brass doors of the Sheraton Towers Singapore were merely a flirtation compared to the hotel's opulent interior. I had never laid eyes on such architectural beauty. My room resembled a chamber for a princess, with walnut- and teak-paneled walls, fresh orchids by the bed, and ice already in the bucket by the mini-bar. I had never stayed in a room so magnificent. Even the glass by the bathroom sink was lead crystal. The robe in the closet was a pristine, frothy poof of cotton that smelled faintly like white plumeria. My heart fluttered. I couldn't believe I was in exotic Singapore! Not many people get to see this magical land or experience the sumptuous Sheraton Towers Singapore. I was in heaven.

The restaurant menu was tantalizing. I resolved to try each appetizer—no matter how exotic—and to order a Singapore Sling at the bar. After following through on all counts, and having no idea what I'd eaten, I returned to my room, exhausted, sated, and happy. I crawled into bed hoping my ship would never arrive—but arrive it did, one day later.

The next morning the agent collected me and we drove to the refinery where I would join the ship, which was taking on a new cargo of jet fuel.

When we arrived at the gate, a short, stocky guard informed us, in the most officious tone he could muster in his broken English, that even though my name was on the access list, and despite the fact I was the ship's new second officer, I would not be permitted to join the ship. I must have looked at least mildly perplexed, because he inhaled deeply and went on to explain, with tilted head and helpless upturned palms, that although I was on the crew list, I was not allowed on refinery grounds, because I was...er...a woman. He didn't see how I could get to the ship. Silly me—what was I thinking?

Now what to do? The two men started gesticulating and chattering in increasingly high-pitched tones. Funny thing I noticed about men that night. American men get louder when they get frustrated; Asian men raise their pitch. Anyway, I had to get to the ship. The security truck was the only transportation authorized to access the docks. Sitting in the cab was out of the question, even if I were to be completely concealed.

After much wrangling and gnashing of teeth, I finally convinced the guard to smuggle me in his pickup truck. By now, the poor man was a mess. Given Singapore's Draconian legal system, I understood why he was sweating so profusely and was so afraid of losing his job.

It was decided that the only way he'd transport me was to smuggle me to the ship in an empty 55-gallon drum sitting on the bed of the little security pick-up truck. At least then he might be able to claim he didn't know I was there, if we were to get caught. The drum was empty but not very clean. At this point, I didn't care. I climbed in—he tossed an oily burlap sack over me—and off we went, bouncing down the refinery road to deliver the ship's new second officer to her ship.

I can only imagine what the crewman on the ship's gangway thought when an oily girl emerged from a 55-gallon drum on the bed of the security truck.

Executing such a dramatic arrival at the gangway really broke the ice, and made me somewhat of a folk hero aboard that ship.

6

It *All* Matters:
How to Behave

"Provocative Uniform" by Stephen C. Coutts

♂♀♂

As a cadet, recruit, trainee, apprentice, or new employee, your reputation is just starting to form. Your career and the foundation of your reputation started the day you began your training.

In every culture, there exist norms and standards of polite behavior. Not exhibiting these behaviors will almost certainly take you out of the running for advanced positions and opportunities, and you'll never even know it. I see no downside and every advantage to learning etiquette and the social rules of both your own culture and those of any countries you may be visiting. Your behavior, your bearing, and your demeanor will label you—fairly or not—with regard to education, socio-economic level, and intelligence.

"Having class" is a behavior easily learned, and which has little to do with wealth or formal education. Some of the most boorish people I know are wealthy and educated.

Give yourself every advantage, especially in a masculine environment where you will be under intense scrutiny, by exhibiting proper, gracious, and classy behavior. As I said, your reputation will stick to you like glue, so make it as favorable as possible.

The same people you knew as a student or new recruit will be the peer group with whom you will advance through the ranks. Years later, your nicknames and reputation will be remembered—often in the most unforgiving context.

The pot doesn't get stirred much in specialized fields, and we women really stick out. If a guy dances naked on a barroom table, it will be remembered, but it is far more memorable—and permanently damaging—for a woman who does so. I see my classmates at conferences, awards ceremonies, and aboard ship now, working as captains and very senior managers. We're the same people—a bit older and fatter now—but a lot smarter. I'd like to share some of the "smarter" with you.

Private Behavior Matters

A youthful misconception I hear frequently these days is that young people think if they are good at their jobs, no one cares how they spend their free time. "Our free time is our business," they argue. They believe that how they spend their free time is not their employers', schools', or their military units' concern.

If you share this misconception, here are two stories that might broaden your perspective. Hopefully you will learn that every decision comes with a price, and that every action bears a consequence. Some may be worth the price and some may not be, but never assume that what you do "off the clock" doesn't matter. It *all* matters.

Lisa Nowak, a graduate of the U.S. Naval Academy, was a NASA astronaut. According to widely published news reports, in 2007 she was accused of driving over 1,000 miles and attacking her romantic rival, a woman who reportedly was dating an astronaut with whom, allegedly, Ms. Nowak also had romantic interests. As a result of her actions, and to avoid harsher charges, Ms. Nowak pled guilty to burglary and battery in 2009.[9] When the news media flashed her mug shot, it was often next to her official NASA astronaut portrait.

Think NASA cared? Ms. Nowak was, after all, off the clock and not officially representing NASA. I dare say NASA cared. I would imagine the U.S. Naval Academy cared, too. I would bet her hometown, her parents, her siblings, her high school, and everyone who had a personal or professional connection to her cared very much about her behavior off the clock. Why? Because it reflected on them.

Another story makes the point even clearer. Picture an exceedingly competent corporate tax attorney. She is a bit on fashion's wild side. She sports various piercings (both visible and not), and likes to alternate hair colors on weekends. She is embellished with multiple tattoos, none of which are visible in business attire. For work, she dresses conservatively and removes all visible piercings. During the week, her hair is a natural color, and is worn in a professional style. She works at a major law firm and is being considered for partner.

Two weeks before the partners are to meet, she is pushing her shopping cart through a market, when whom does she bump into, but her supervising attorney. She is on her own time, in her own town, and is in her casual style with blue hair, the piercings in her face installed, and is wearing short shorts and a tank top that reveal her tattoos. Ultimately, she is passed over for partner.

She would never know whether the chance meeting with her superior tipped the scales against her. You must admit, her clothing, piercings, and tattoos most likely did not give her an advantage.

In the U.S., for the most part, you have the right to dress as you wish on your own time, and to poke holes in your body, and to draw permanently on your skin. No one is alleging otherwise. Recognize that employers, in turn, have the right to protect their reputations, and to hire and promote people they feel share their corporate values and who will reflect positively on their firms.

I recall heated debates about President Clinton's alleged ex-tracurricular activities with one of his aides. Many of my friends felt that what a person did on his own free time was nobody's business. I argued that what an elected official does on his own time is absolutely everyone's business, since what a person does on his own time, especially if he thinks no one is looking, is the only true measure of character.

Americans are uniquely free to be reckless with our freedoms, and we often don't appreciate the long-term consequences of our actions. What you do on the clock is regulated by your employer. What you do off the clock is justifiably used as an indicator of your maturity, character, and your decision-making ability. Don't be surprised or upset if people judge you more on your use of your private, discretionary time than on what you do at work, where you are being told what to do. We all have twenty-four hours to spend each day, some of which are discretionary. How you choose to spend your discretionary free time is up to you. But never as-sume no one is paying attention or that no one cares. They *are* paying attention and they *do* care.

"Unexpected Boss" by Stephen C. Coutts

Beware Recordings and Nicknames

Unfortunately, many of your indiscretions may be remembered, even recorded, long after you have matured and forgotten all about them. One cadet had the unfortunate distinction of being on the anchor brake of the training ship's windlass when we lost the anchor in the very deep water just off Easter Island. Though he was not responsible for the loss, to this day he is known as "Ten-Shot," that being the length of chain that was lost. (A shot is ninety feet.)

A recent female graduate from my institution had the unfortunate nickname "mattress back," upon which I'll not elaborate. It's doubly unfortunate that even we faculty got wind of the moniker. Hopefully, your nickname(s) will be more flattering.

Reputations take a long time to build, but mere seconds to destroy. Unlike in my youth, when times were much more forgiving, these days everyone is armed with a ready camera or video device. With the advent of social networking sites such as YouTube®, MySpace®, and Facebook®, the Internet enables the dissemination of images around the world in an instant. These images are, for all practical purposes, permanent.

Employers are not stupid. It is now considered routine due diligence to search the Internet for information on prospective candidates and to scour the social sites when doing background checks. Even if you have removed images from your own site(s), they may have been posted elsewhere. Having unflattering images on the Internet is like tearing open a feather pillow. It can never be 100% restored and the damage can last forever. You can't put squeezed toothpaste back in the tube.

There are consequences, good and bad, for every decision you make. My advice to you is, don't do anything stupid in public. Better yet, don't do stupid things at all.

Workspace and Personal Space Cleanliness

When I was single and dating, one of my secret tests was how clean and well maintained a man kept his car. I figured if a man didn't maintain his vehicle, he was either too poor to maintain it, too sloppy, or too lazy—none of which were traits of the man I hoped to marry. I didn't care whether the car was expensive or not, just that it was well-maintained and clean. I could extrapolate from a man's vehicle how he maintained his house, and even his personal affairs. I would instantly write off a slob. It didn't mean he was a bad person, or dull, or stupid, or poor. It meant he would have been a bad match for me.

Employers and supervisors think the same way. Even if your superior keeps an office that looks like it was ravaged by a hurricane, don't think that your being neat, clean, and organized isn't a desirable trait. It is—especially to a disorganized supervisor.

You can give yourself an advantage by ensuring you keep not just your workspace clean, but by keeping your personal spaces, including your car, tidy as well.

While we're on the subject of cars, if you must have bumper stickers, I recommend against having anything but the most benign bumper stickers and license plate frames on your car.

Your particular message may set your boss's teeth on edge, or alienate someone who might have been a valuable resource, mentor, or ally. Would you be excited about hiring a woman who had a license frame that read "First Class Bitch"?

The same advice can be extended to workspace decorations, such as calendars, posters, and pictures. If you have a kitten calendar or a fuzzy-wuzzy key fob, don't be surprised if no one recommends you for sniper school.

Such inferences are not necessarily fair, and perhaps such behaviors shouldn't matter—but they do.

Handwriting, Spelling, and Grammar

I have been teaching college for fifteen years, and I am increasingly horrified by the writing skills of most college students. It doesn't matter how brilliant the message, if the writer can't transmit the message effectively because his or her handwriting, spelling, or grammar is so bad it distracts the reader, the message is lost.

A college senior e-mailed me once to ask whether he was "aloud" to take his notes into an exam. The word is correctly spelled, just incorrectly used, so most e-mail or word processing applications' spell-check features wouldn't have caught his error.

I believe young people are now so accustomed to texting, e-mailing, and writing in obscure acronyms and abbreviations, that the language centers of their brains have atrophied and turned to mush. Writing e-mail matters as much as writing on paper. Consider e-mail messages your work product, as you would a paper memo.

If you have poor handwriting, you absolutely must work to make it legible. If you are a poor speller, make the effort to have someone proofread anything you plan on sending out to the universe.

When I read a student's poor writing, I almost automatically assume the student is not as bright as his classmate whose writing is legible, whose words are correctly used and spelled, and thus, whose meaning is clear.

If I were hiring someone, it ~~wood~~ would matter ~~two too~~ to me that they knew *new* from *knew*!

If you are weak in this area, regardless of whether your facts are accurate, the reader will probably assume that you are not very intelligent. The best way to get your language skills up to par is to read good books. Reading newspapers probably won't be as helpful, but it's better than reading nothing at all. Ideally, you should always be reading a culturally defining, good book.[10]

Books define our culture. They are woven into the fabric of our society by way of jokes, stories, and anecdotes. If you are not well-read, certain jokes or references will go right over your head. You won't absorb as much meaning and nuance from the expressions of others. With a merely functional vocabulary and only one's own experiences from which to draw, life would indeed be dull. For example, if you're at a cocktail party and a fellow party guest remarks that he feels like he just "fell down a rabbit hole," you wouldn't understand the reference unless you had read *Alice in Wonderland*. Well-read people luxuriate in the nuance of reading about a crimson sunset, rather than just a red one. Reading substantive books will enrich your life, and give your experiences increased depth and perspective.

Remember, you are a minority in an alien environment. Everything you do will be scrutinized and judgments will be made about you based on scant information. It's not fair. Whoever said there is a double standard obviously couldn't count—there are many more than just two!

Do yourself a favor—learn the difference between "to" and "too," "their," "there," and "they're," and the many other English-language peculiarities that often confuse people.

Current Events

A faculty colleague of mine has a highly educated, very intelligent son who didn't get selected for a desirable job. According to my colleague, her son is convinced the reason he didn't get the job is that he didn't stay informed of important current events. Someone at his luncheon interview had brought up events in Russia that had been in the news, and her son couldn't even begin to comment. It was an awkward moment as he sat there, silent, with all eyes upon him. For want of a nail, the kingdom was lost![11]

See? If you don't know the anecdote of horseshoes and nails, you have no idea what I'm talking about. I'm not suggesting you become a game show champion. I'm suggesting that you become a well-read, well-informed citizen of the planet.

If your goal is to progress up the ranks, you will have to be smart and aware. Depending on your field, you may have to be smarter and more aware than your male counterparts, just to be considered equal. In my opinion, the newer women are to an industry, the better their performance will have to be to reach an even footing with the men. You may have to excel intellectually to merely be considered average.

To stay up to date, read better periodicals, especially those particular to your business or industry. Read what your boss reads. Ask respected colleagues what they read to keep informed and current.

Remember, you will never know about opportunities you are not offered. You will never receive a rejection letter explaining *why* you weren't selected—you'll just be politely rejected. While much progress has been made in many industries and in the military to "level the playing field," it will never be level. If you are in a position from which you want to progress and move up, you will have to bolster your intellectual muscles and global awareness.

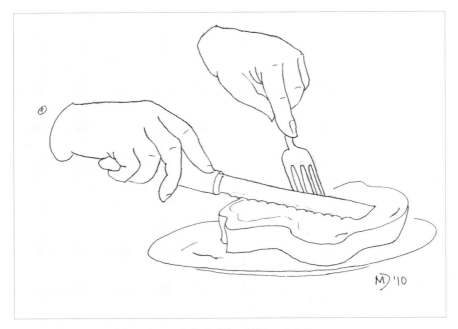

"Continental Style" by Michael J. Durnan

Table Manners

Whether you are working on an oil rig or crouching in a foxhole, someone is watching you. Having table manners, even in environments where you may be the only one who doesn't clench a fork like a spear, may be the tiny straw that tips the scales in your favor for a promotion, bonus, or other wonderful opportunity.

To even be considered for a position one must be fundamentally qualified, so it is often the little things that set one candidate apart from another—in either a good way or a bad way. Suzanne Giesemann, a former navy commander, was selected to serve as aide-de-camp to the Chairman of the Joint Chiefs of Staff. Why was she selected for this position above all others? Only her employer knows for certain. Obviously, something she did impressed the right person and it was probably several little, but important things that set her apart.

Table manners are a learned skill which, if ignored, could result in a rejected application, or a wonderful opportunity never being brought to your attention. Sometimes jobs aren't posted at all, and candidates aren't recruited. When people in power want to hire a person who displays desirable behaviors or skills, they often can create a suitable position where none existed before.

When I say "table manners" I am not talking about dipping in finger bowls or sniffing wine corks. I mean the simple, basic handling of utensils, the use of napkins, and respecting social mores. Learning basic table manners will give you an advantage.[12]

I first noticed an acute lack of social graces in today's young people when I started inviting cadets to my home for steak dinners. It's not that I'm generous—I had a motive for inviting them.

Years ago, I gave an examination in celestial navigation, on which almost all of my students missed the same question. I was perplexed. Upon checking their calculations, I realized they had all used an incorrect sign in a lengthy formula. When I went back to check my lecture notes, sure enough, my formula had the wrong sign. I had infected all of their notes when I put the erroneous formula from my notes on the board.

At the next session, I asked the class why, since the correct formula was in the text, none of them had reported my error. They said I was intimidating; they didn't want to contradict me in class. I was taken aback. I realized I had to do something.

I initiated a tradition of inviting those students who catch me making substantive errors in class to my house for a big steak dinner with all the trimmings. After the first year, word got out that these weren't any sissy steaks either!

Now, my lectures are like treasure hunts for the students. Not only do I have classes full of eager cadets trying diligently to catch me making a mistake on the board, but my lecture notes get sanitized every semester! It is a win-win situation.

I am confident that when I had these clever cadets to my home for dinner, they were on their best behavior, but I was shocked by their lack of basic table manners. I finally commented on it and, in the gentlest of ways, proceeded to show them how to hold knife and fork, with something other than a Neanderthal death-grip.

They all seemed grateful and a little peeved that their own parents hadn't shown them the ropes. They didn't even know little things, such as the common courtesy of pushing one's chair back under a table after rising. I was thrilled they could now survive an interview luncheon and not be eliminated immediately due to bad table manners.

This may not apply to every dining situation, but you should know the basics. Even in a rough-and-tumble masculine world, table manners can only enhance your reputation. Here are a few pointers.

First, napkins go onto your lap when you sit down—definitely before you start eating.

Unless you're at a buffet or large banquet, it is generally considered proper to wait until everyone is served before starting to eat. Unless told otherwise, the senior person at the table should start eating first.

Never chew with your mouth open. Don't speak with food in your mouth.

There are two styles of handling knife and fork: the American style and the Continental style.

Interestingly, the Continental style is more common in the United States. In the Continental style, the fork is held tines down in the left hand while the knife is held in the right. After the food has been cut, the fork, without a change in hand position, is brought to the mouth tines down.

In the American style, after the food has been cut, the knife is set down on the edge of the plate, blade inward; the fork is shifted to the right hand and is brought to the mouth tines up.

Elbows do not belong on tables. I am terrible at this, especially if the chairs have no arms, but it is considered impolite.

Never use the communal butter knife to spread butter on your bread or roll. When the butter plate reaches you, use the communal knife to slice off as much butter as you'll need, and place the butter on your plate. Then pass the butter and knife to the next person. To eat your bread, tear off a bite-sized portion (never slather the whole roll with butter), and butter it using your personal butter knife.

There are many other rules of polite behavior, in far too much detail for the scope of this book. Do yourself the service of at least knowing what the rules are. You can then choose to use them or not, as the situation merits.

Posture

My husband and I were in the lobby of an upscale hotel in Reno, Nevada, where I noticed a well-dressed family with three teen-aged sons, relaxing on couches around a large coffee table. The mother appeared well appointed, with a large diamond ring, fine jewelry, and well-tailored, tasteful clothes. The father, equally well-dressed and well-groomed, looked to be about forty-five years old. To my astonishment, the father had his feet up on the table, as did two of the boys. I was appalled, but of course didn't breathe a word to anyone. I was hoping the hotel personnel would ask them to remove their feet from the furniture, but in the hospitality trades the "customer is always right"—so of course, nothing happened.

When I was young, I was taught in no uncertain terms to keep my feet off furniture. As children, if we transgressed, the nearest adult would invariably bark, "Get your feet off the furniture! Were you raised in a barn?" What has happened to our culture?

The family I saw at the hotel, no matter how wealthy or how schooled, lacked class. If asked, I would never recommend them for anything. Luckily the man wasn't wearing his employer's uniform!

I have seen women sit with their legs spread wide apart. Even in dirty overalls or fatigues, this is unseemly and unnecessary. I know it's not the end of the world if a woman sits that way, but she may be doing herself just that tiny disservice that sends a signal that she is coarse, or sexually available, or at best, doesn't come from a gracious household. Knowing nothing about a woman, would you, upon seeing her in such a posture, default toward the positive and assume she was highly educated and intelligent? Be honest!

These assumptions may not be fair, or even accurate, but who told you life and human reactions are fair? We all generate opinions almost instantly. We all categorize people as friend or foe, rich or poor, smart or stupid, and as having many other characteristics—often unconsciously. I want to convey to you how important the little things can be, so that you will train yourself to behave in ways that will enhance your life and afford you every advantage. I wish someone had told me these things when I was younger—I'll never know what I might have missed.

Handshakes

I am constantly stunned and disappointed by the limp handshakes I get from otherwise robust young men. It used to be that ladies would not shake hands, but instead would proffer a hand for a polite kiss. Nowadays, a lady's handshake should be just as sound as a gentleman's. Handshakes should be pleasantly firm, not death grips, and in our culture, solid, pleasant eye contact should be maintained. In some cultures, eye contact is considered rude.

Some men, especially politicians and those trying to sell you something, like to cradle your right elbow, or otherwise touch you with their left hand while they shake your right hand. I have always found this disconcerting and inappropriate, but never felt it worth doing anything about. I would immediately have my antenna up, and be wary if someone took this approach with me.

Wearing the nametag on the right side of the chest facilitates its reading during a handshake. Some cultures don't use handshakes, or don't use them with women; so don't take immediate offense if, when you're overseas, a native doesn't shake your hand, but does shake a man's.

I have had the misfortune of shaking hands with men who felt I didn't belong, and they would indicate their displeasure with me by giving me a bone-crushing squeeze, and watching eagerly for my reaction. Sensing the squeeze coming on, I would squeeze right back. If this happens to you, recognize this as rude, childish behavior, but it's not worth making a scene over. Just mark the guy off your "good guy" list and get on with your meeting. At least you've been alerted—the guy is a jerk.

Answering Phones

Many organizations, especially the military, have a specific way one is supposed to answer phones. If your organization does not have an official policy, it may be wise to ask what the expectation is at work.

Your home phone and cell phone greetings and messages should be mature and appropriate. Having a lame "Yo, whaddup?" greeting, or music, or a cutie-pie type of message won't impress anyone, and may even hamper your career. Now that you are in the work world, everything you expose to the universe should be mature and professional.

Some women, for safety reasons, may enlist a male friend to record their outgoing greeting, or they may just use the voicemail system's default voice, which is what I did when I was single.

When you leave a message, it is considered courteous to always leave your phone number, slowly and clearly, at the beginning of the message, as well as at the end. That way, if the number is missed, the person won't have to listen to the entire message again, just to retrieve the number.

Ensure that your e-mail signatures are appropriate for your aspirations. If you're hoping to be promoted to police chief or admiral, having frilly wallpaper on your e-mail messages probably won't enhance your odds. You may even want to establish two e-mail personalities, one for work and one for personal use.

Always Do Just a Little Extra

My husband and I were shopping for a boatyard to perform work on our sailboat. We were trying to find the least expensive yard for the jobs we wanted done. On a lark, we decided to check out the fanciest, most expensive yard in the area.

It was nearly closing time when we arrived. Workers were starting to head back to the main building to clean up and go home. It was a windy, chilly day, and as we approached the doorway, we could see part of the yard through the fence. A foam cup had been blown out of an overflowing garbage can, and scudded along the asphalt. A worker, clearly done for the day, walked out of his way, chased down the cup, and put it into the garbage can, tamping it down so it wouldn't be blown out again. This worker's attention to detail and his work ethic, especially since he didn't know anyone was watching, immediately impressed us both.

Guess which yard we use now—and all because a worker picked up an errant cup.

Another thing the "fancy" yard does right is something my husband taught me. They under-promise and over-deliver. In law school, we did an exercise that illustrated the point, but didn't have such a cool phrase to describe it. Here's how it went.

A person approaches two banks in search of a mortgage loan. One bank says they will have an answer back by 5:00 p.m. at the latest, and the second bank says they'll have an answer back by 3:00 p.m. The first bank calls at 3:00 p.m., two hours early, and gives the customer the quote. The second bank, unable to get through at 3:00 p.m. because the line was busy, finally gets through at 3:15 p.m. Now, which bank do you think made the more favorable impression? They both performed at basically the same time.

This practice is similar to how a clever salesman or contractor will always come in just under their estimate. That way, because the customer was prepared for a higher number, he or she is more likely to be satisfied with the final cost.

Some managers have a habit of *requesting* tasks be done, rather than *telling* someone to do something. Young people often respond to these requests as though they really are requests. They usually are not. For most people in supervisory and leadership positions, a suggestion is just a nice way of giving an assignment.

People of my vintage often assume a younger person will understand that such a request is not really a request. We expect that a subordinate will hop to it and get it done. Our logic is, "There's no time like the present!" and "Make hay while the sun shines!" If you wait until the task is convenient for you, it may be interpreted as lazy, indifferent, or even incompetent or insolent.

When anyone superior to you requests or suggests that you do something, jump on it. Don't let the polite tone fool you— they are expecting an immediate response. Times used to be so much more genteel. A polite hint was all that was needed to get a person off their duff and working. With many young people these days, I feel as though I need to clap them upside the head to get them moving! It didn't used to be this way, and it isn't in many foreign cultures. Such behavior may indicate someone doesn't understand or appreciate the global competition they will be facing as they enter the work world.

Don't put yourself in positions in which you promise more than you can deliver. Always leave every space better off for your having been there. If someone makes a passing remark that something should be done, jump on it and get it done.

Always do just a little extra—just the tiniest thing can make a difference. As a woman in a "man's world" you will be under much more scrutiny than your male colleagues. Fair or not, you will have to shine twice as bright for half the credit. Trust me—it is the little things that matter most.

7

Wear Not to Flirt:
Grooming and Clothing

"No Respect" by Philomena "Phil" Sulzen

Clothing makes a powerful statement. Clothes indicate the level of importance you assign to another person, an event, or a setting. Even on a scorching, hot day, most gracious and sane people wouldn't wear a bathrobe to a job interview or a bikini to a funeral. But why not? Really? Why shouldn't people just be comfortable and wear what they want no matter what the occasion?

First off, that's not our culture (thank goodness we have some culture left). Second, in every culture, clothes send important, powerful, and easily recognized social messages. How can one, at a distance, instantly distinguish a doctor from a nurse? Clothes. A thug from a businessman? Clothes. A flirtatious woman from one more reserved? Clothes. How does one distinguish law enforcement? Clothes. You see—clothing matters.

Some experts say that most communication is conveyed visually, not vocally. Clothing and appearances convey information about you—especially when you are relatively new and have no history, nor any sort of good reputation, preceding you to the job.

Work Clothes

Almost all companies either require a uniform or have established some sort of dress codes. If there is no official dress code, dress like respected co-workers dress. Many jobs require personal protective equipment (PPE). My best advice regarding work clothes is to wear the type of garb worn by those equal or senior to you.

Petroleum handling positions almost all require Nomex® overalls, and prohibit the wearing of nylon windbreakers and other types of clothes that generate static electricity. Nomex is hot and uncomfortable, so I always wore a crew-neck cotton undershirt and cotton boxers or shorts underneath to keep the Nomex off my skin. Be sure to find out what the requirements of your job are before you leave, so you can bring the right work clothes.

Most industrial work sites require steel-toed leather boots. Some require boots with a heel, rather than a flat sole, as they are considered safer on ladders. Some require lace-up rather than pull-on boots, because they are easier to remove after an injury. Some companies also require the soles to be oil resistant. Again, ask what specific clothing your position requires, if any.

Buy good thick socks and boots that fit well. Bring extra insoles. Don't skimp. Women get foot rot as easily as men. I always wore shower sandals in the showers, despite my routine of dousing the pan with bleach.

Take your own work gloves. The gloves available from most employers will fit you like a sleeping bag. I have had the best luck buying leather gardening gloves. Take several pairs. Also carry a supply of the cheap, disposable cotton gloves often found at flea markets and everywhere in the Far East.

Take your own knife and several flashlights. I always carried a Leatherman® multi-tool, a wicked sharp knife (which I would make a point of leisurely sharpening during coffee breaks), a small spiral notebook that would fit in my breast pocket, a black pen, and a small but powerful flashlight. Of all the items you carry, it is the knife or the multi-tool that may save your life or the life of a co-worker. Keep the knife sharp. Serrated blades generally do better at cutting line than straight blades. Be sure the blade locks. Many marine and rigger's knives don't have locking blades, which I consider dangerous.

If you must wear a helmet or hardhat, consider investing in terrycloth liners for the headband. I would take several.

I always took my own safety goggles and glasses. They are different. Goggles wrap all the way around the eye area and have an elastic band; safety glasses are like sunglasses. You can get shatter-proof glasses at sporting goods stores and gun shops. I'd have both clear and tinted. You will inevitably lose or crush a pair. Some people like the glasses tethered around their neck. Invest in at least two good pair of polarized sunglasses and a neck tether. You will lose one!

If you're headed to sunny climates, one of my favorite items was a hat that looked like a ball cap, but had a flap I could lower to protect the sides and back of my neck. It was a neck-saver.

Casual Clothes

It is generally a bad idea to wear anything in the workplace that might alienate someone else, especially when you are new or in a junior position. For example, wearing a political T-shirt or button, an overtly religious phrase or icon, or garb supporting various causes can make others uncomfortable and possibly make them think less of your abilities, especially if they disagree with your position. It's just human nature.

Most people are more comfortable around like-minded individuals. When you're new, it's best to keep your political inclinations to yourself. Do your best to politely dodge charged questions such as whom you voted for, whether you think abortion should be legal, etc., by saying you prefer not to discuss politics at work, or some other gracious exit that conceals your position. These topics involve deeply held convictions and could foster ill will or, worse, incite arguments, when discussed with the relative strangers you live and work with. You definitely don't want to tick off your superiors—and you just never know who may spit in your coffee pot. I've seen it happen. Remember, you'll be working with these people for a long time.

For recreation and off-hours, your best interests will be served if you avoid dressing provocatively. While you may be young, pretty, and as hot as Georgia asphalt, the workplace is not the appropriate venue to wile your charms.

It has always bothered me when women who wear provocative clothing get upset (or pretend to get upset) when a man notices. It wasn't that a man noticed—it was that the *wrong* man noticed. If you're wearing neon, don't complain about being mistaken for an "open" sign.

The men probably are tiptoeing around because of you already, so don't make their workplace even more uncomfortable by turn-

"Real Men" by Philomena "Phil" Sulzen

ing yourself into a fishing lure that's hard to ignore. Dress casually and comfortably. Hot pants, low-cut tops that emphasize cleavage, anything see-through, too tight, or overly lacy will not enhance your reputation and will make the men around you uncomfortable. One of my male colleagues feels that even darts in a blouse are inappropriate, as they tend to accentuate the bust.

We had a rule for our teenage daughter's clothing. I would drop a quarter down her shirt or jeans, and if it didn't fall through, the clothes were too tight. If we could read the date on the quarter through her jeans, or see the outline of a bra strap through her shirt, the clothes were definitely too tight!

I am appalled by the modern affliction of wearing bedroom slippers and pajamas in public. This is in exceedingly bad taste and indicates a flippant, immature, dismissive attitude. This behavior silently screams that the wearer could care less about the opinions of others. It is a sign of disrespect and to my sensibilities, a way of "flipping off," in the rudest possible way, the dignity of our culture and our social norms.

While watching coverage of the earthquake in Haiti, I observed newly destitute women ironing their clothes on slabs of concrete rubble, such was their personal pride.

When I see young people wearing pajamas in public, no matter how appropriately they may be dressed when I see them later, I have already formed a less than flattering opinion of them. I would be unlikely to recommend them for anything, no matter how smart they may be.

I assume that young people who dress like that have probably never experienced any real hardships in their lives. When I travel overseas and see truly poor people, they usually have more dignity, more pride in themselves, and more respect for their culture than to intentionally dress in such a slovenly manner.

For everyday footwear when not working, it is generally imprudent to wear open-toed shoes aboard any vessel or when going to town. Some companies have policies on footwear. In town, you just never know what you're going to step in, or when you may need to run. Wear appropriate shoes.

If you are feeling your femininity slowly erode, what I used to do, especially when my job had me in greasy overalls every day, was to wear really feminine under-garments and lacy bras. I kept my feminine side nourished, but kept it to myself. Despite my hands being irreversibly stained with crude oil, I made sure my toenails were always polished.

Piercings and Tattoos

To many supervisors and employers, especially in mission critical industries, visible tattoos and piercings are not signs of maturity or sound, independent decision-making. Many men these days call the tattoo women get on the small of their backs a "tramp stamp." Think carefully before permanently inking your body, as your tastes will change with age and tattoos tend to be rather permanent. Will that tattoo be as charming when you're forty? Trust me—your tastes will change. Tattoo removal is painful and expensive, and the scars can be unsightly. (If you must mark yourself up, try henna or a magic marker. You can touch yourself up forever if you choose.)

While tattoos and piercings may be more socially accepted today than in years past, I still can't think of a single instance where having a tattoo or piercing would enhance your image with an employer. The best you could hope for is a neutral impact.

Grooming

Hair should be kept under control for safety reasons. When I was a teenager I was a gas station attendant. In those days, station attendants pumped gas and checked oil and other automotive fluids. I was checking the transmission fluid on a car and my long hair got caught in the running fan belt. That lesson literally yanked me up short.

Be aware of how you smell. For most women, offensive body odor is not an issue—the opposite is. Strong perfumes and colognes don't belong in the workplace. Some people are very allergic, but more importantly it reflects on your professionalism. Your best image will be made wearing no perfume or very light, clean scents. Sometimes even a hint of perfume can generate an unintended impact on a male co-worker.

Aboard ship once, I was getting along just fine with everyone when literally overnight, a shipmate began acting standoffish

"Bad News" by Stephen C. Coutts

towards me. I finally asked him what was going on. It turned out I was using the same scented hair conditioner as his wife and he was having a hard time with it. Men can be sensitive creatures. You should be too. Men get lonely just like you do.

Keep nails short or the worksite will shorten them for you, usually in a most painful way. Black, glittery, or neon colored nail polish won't enhance your professional appearance. Wear it at your peril. Little painted daises on your nails don't scream cutting-edge professionalism either.

Jewelry

Wearing jewelry in an industrial workplace and especially aboard ship is rarely prudent. Some companies have policies restricting it. Certainly, the military does. Rings scratch the delicate screens of electronic instruments. Rings catch on ladder rungs and can tear off a finger if you fall. Crushing a finger with a ring on it is multiples worse than crushing a bare finger. Rings are also excellent conductors of electricity. Many engineers will not wear rings, for just this reason.

Earrings should never be dangling. I even refrain from wearing stud earrings when I'm aboard ship. Necklaces can and will catch on every conceivable bit of hardware, unless well tucked in: the same applies to bracelets.

Jewelry is a physical adornment, and adornments are designed primarily to enhance appearance. Enhancing one's appearance, and trying to be more sexually attractive while working in a masculine environment will nibble away at your credibility. If you must wear jewelry, be modest and safe.

Watches, on the other hand, are critical. I always carried a spare. I bought inexpensive, water-proof digital watches that had a light and an alarm function and a non-metallic band. Even watches with a web or plastic strap would sometimes trigger a rash on my wrist, as chemicals and grit would get trapped under the band. When that happened, I'd have to thread my watch through a belt loop, instead of wear it on my wrist. Tankers and other chemically-laden workplaces may have policies prohibiting pens, watches, and other metallic objects, as they could cause a spark if dropped or struck.

Violating a clothing policy is a sure way to get fired. Be sure you understand what personal protective equipment is required. Comply with the company's rules religiously.

Medical Issues

A dear friend and colleague of mine once said, "Getting hurt at sea is like getting a limp on the Serengeti Plain." He's so right. Many companies will release you from the job if you are incapacitated and/or can't perform your job for over seventy-two hours. The military has its own procedures. Medical care may be unavailable at remote job sites, and you may be sent home if you get sick or injured.

Most employers maintain some sort of medical repatriation insurance. This insurance will pay the very expensive fees involved with flying someone to appropriate medical facilities or even back to the U.S. on a non-commercial flight, sometimes with medical personnel attending. Ask about such policies and if warranted, purchase your own medical repatriation insurance and/or travelers' insurance for the time you'll be overseas. There are many responsible providers that can be found online, and the costs are minimal.

Health Records

If you have any health issues, consider carrying your medical records with you. Most providers can store your entire medical history on a disk or flash drive. I'd recommend carrying this record with you if you plan on being overseas for any length of time, no matter how briefly.

Immunizations and Bugs

Be sure you are up to date on all immunizations recommended for the part of the world you'll be visiting.[13] There used to be a yellow card available from the government to record all your immunizations. Today, a simple print-out from your health care provider listing all your immunizations will usually suffice. Be sure to carry a copy with you. Consider visiting the Centers for Disease

Control (CDC) web site to learn about any health hazards at your destination. You may want to pack insect repellent if you expect to be in buggy countries. I never expected the employer to give me a tutorial on these matters. I always did my own homework when traveling.

Living Will

Consider drafting a living will, if you haven't already. This document guides decision-makers regarding your wishes in medical emergencies. Most health care providers have forms you can complete, and leave on record with your loved ones and your employer. If you will be overseas for a long time, carry a copy with you.

8

My First Stabbing:
Discouraging Romantic Advances

"My First Stabbing" by Michael J. Durnan

The with whom it is appropriate to socialize will differ from industry to industry, and from company to company. The military has strict rules concerning fraternization, as do some companies. Many social rules are unwritten. Recognize that the unwritten rules are different for female-male interactions than for same-sex relationships.

I hope my advice will help you avoid sideways glances and rumors. I hope my advice will help you maintain your reputation as a professional, who happens to be female. Remember, the rules, like life, aren't fair, but you chose a profession that will be a wonderful adventure if you play by the rules—especially the unwritten ones.

Fraternization

Fraternization rules arose from necessity. Bosses and superiors are the ones assigning jobs, writing evaluations, ordering people into burning buildings, war zones, crime scenes, and other situations where favoritism, or even the appearance of favoritism, must be avoided at all costs. Fraternization may cloud one's judgment and hamper one's decision-making abilities. Inappropriate fraternization also creates tension amongst your colleagues.

Aboard most commercial and naval ships, officers eat and sleep in separate areas from the unlicensed crew and/or enlisted sailors, but this is not always the case. I sailed on a Wallenius Lines car carrier where officers and crew dined together and would even play cards together after dinner. That ship was unusual also in that all crew—both officers and unlicensed—were allowed to bring their spouses to ride aboard. It was a very civilized ship.

Tugs, supply vessels, and other "brown water" craft are usually more casual, and may have different norms of behavior than deep-sea vessels. Naval vessels have clear rules regarding fraternization, as do most military, law enforcement, and firefighting workplaces. Other industrial employers may or may not have express rules regarding fraternization.

Your best bet is to observe carefully and to behave as your superiors and respected peers do. An even safer tactic, if you have any doubts, is to ask your immediate supervisor when you first report for duty. This may really impress him or her that you are sensitive to these issues and will not stretch company expectations. When in doubt, always err on the side of conservative behaviors.

Going to Town with a Male Colleague

As (usually) the only female aboard, going ashore for me was often a lonely proposition. Military bases and naval vessels have many more people, so this is rarely an issue for service personnel. On a hard-working merchant vessel, there may only be a few people who are off when you are and with whom you could go ashore. This may be true of other workplaces as well, especially those working around the clock with some sort of shift system. Obviously your co-workers are usually men who often don't want to do what you want to do when you go into town. The bigger issue is that of "appearances."

The image of a lone female heading into town with a male gives the appearance of impropriety, no matter how innocent. I advise against it. Trust me. I know how lonely it can be. In many ports, I simply didn't go ashore, because there was no one appropriate for me to go with and I didn't feel safe going alone. Instead, I would watch a movie. The best bet is to go into town with a group. If there's another lady around, go with her or, as a last resort, another male of equal status. Going into town or meeting up with a single man just begs for rumors to start and reputations to bud.

Aboard my first ship, I was befriended by Paul, the second mate. Perhaps "befriended" isn't the right word. More accurately, he took pity on me.

The ship was a small, rusty, jet fuel tanker in the South China Sea. It was fishing season in that region. One foggy night, the radar, even on very low scales, had so many contacts it looked as though someone had spilled a bag of frozen peas on the screen. The captain was a miserable, greasy, fat Italian who would yell at me every time I'd call him for help with traffic. He hated girls (which was odd, because he had married one), and he really hated Kings Pointers. Strike two for me. Calling on him when the traffic got too dense was always unpleasant.

"Goddamn it!" he'd holler. "If I have to go up there, what the hell do I need you for?" It was all rather stressful.

Anyway, Paul was a character. He was married to a woman he absolutely adored. He adored her so much, in fact, that when he shipped out, he carried with him a life-sized wall poster of her at the Grand Canyon, naked, sporting two assault rifles, one propped on each hip, and bandoliers strung across her bare breasts. He would gaze at her picture and sigh, "What a woman." His other idol was Jane Goodall, the chimpanzee researcher.

Watch was so stressful that after each watch, I'd return to my cabin and vomit. It wasn't the food. It was the stress. I could hold it together for the four-hour watch, but that was it. It got so bad I was beginning to think I just wasn't cut out for the job. I finally confided in Paul.

"Don't worry about it," Paul said, waving his hand dismissively. "I used to throw up all the time on this run." He was a godsend. Eventually I stopped throwing up and was able to get through a night without calling the captain.

It so happened that the only other person off when I was off in port was Paul, so we'd head into town together to shop for anything we needed and grab a meal ashore. No one said anything to me. I had no hint of any impropriety or warnings about appearances. When it was time for Paul to go home, his wife met him on the dock.

The boatswain (the senior unlicensed deck crewman) was standing around waiting for a cab. He made a snide comment to Paul's wife about Paul "playing" with me for the last four months, how we always went ashore together and came back late.

"Just Friends" by Michael J. Durnan

It was a disaster. I can only imagine her initial emotions, the distrust and surprise and the adrenaline shock that must have coursed through her body. I was pretty and young—her husband was a handsome man. We were cooped up together for four months. It was all we could do to convince her that nothing had happened.

Mercy Wright described having similar misunderstandings with her Marine Corps colleagues:

> I pictured myself having a lot of male friends. On top of the fact that I was very outgoing, friendly, young, slim, and attractive, I was also naïve, gullible, and a dreamer. When I graduated from boot camp and went on to my combat training, I was the "pretty" marine with long, dark, curly hair and—out of uniform—a great, girly style.
>
> I can honestly say that even though I did not dress provocatively or inappropriately (because of my spiritual beliefs and values), I still attracted attention from the guys. To an extent, I used this as a tool, but this tool did not always work in my favor…I enjoyed getting girly and pretty after work, and would hang out with the guys. Then when it came to duty or work time, I liked to show off that I could do at least twenty push-ups (not the female version) with the guys in my department when we did morning PT.
>
> Because of my friendliness, I had many men take my personality as flirtatious or my being interested in a 'friends with benefits' program—which was not the case. That had to be nipped right away, and unfortunately, some friendships had to come to an end. That was one of my naïve moments.
>
> I thought I could hang with the guys and not feel the butt of judgment or accusations. In some cases, unfortunately, it's hit or miss: I could either do all the right things and have the wrong (unwanted) outcome, or do all the wrong things and still have the wrong (unwanted) outcome.[14]

These are valuable lessons—ones which I hope you don't have to learn the hard way. Learn from our mistakes and don't behave in ways that can be easily misinterpreted.

Discouraging Romantic Advances

Intimate relationships in the workplace will almost always end badly, and will make everyone around you uncomfortable. Some companies have policies prohibiting intimate relationships between employees, not because the employers are prudes, but because of the increased legal exposure the company faces when such relationships go bad.

Intimate relationships also interfere with managerial decision-making, because the impact of any decision will extend to impact the lover as well, even if indirectly—not to mention the ripples that spread to affect other co-workers. The military has strict rules about such behavior not because they oppose people enjoying each other, but because it erodes operational readiness and unit stability.

Any sort of intimate activity between people in the workplace makes everyone else's job harder—even if the actual "activity" happens away from the jobsite. That's probably why intimacy between colleagues is so resented by others, even in conventional workplaces. It is doubly resented where the female/male ratio is so skewed that only a few very lucky men have any hope of winning female attentions.

Henry Kissinger, a very powerful former U.S. Secretary of State, but not a man usually associated with giving romantic advice, supposedly once said, "Power is the ultimate aphrodisiac." I think he is right. It is natural for women to be attracted to men in powerful positions and it is natural for men to be attracted to ladies. Having romantic relations in the workplace can permanently damage your reputation and career. *Suspected* relationships can be equally damaging.

Fair or not, when it comes to sexual relations in the workplace it is the woman—not the man—who gets labeled a "slut." If the fellow is really, honestly interested in you and you in him, you can indulge the romance after one or both of you have left the job.

Occasionally, even innocent actions can become a problem. During one of my sea tours as a cadet, I had to draw a refrigeration diagram, and for this I needed blueprints. The blueprints were maintained by the reefer engineer, an unlicensed crewman. To get them, I had to go to his cabin and rummage through his filing cabinet. I guess someone saw me, and, by the time the news reached the captain, I allegedly was having a physical relationship with the young reefer engineer.

Unbeknownst to me, this version of the events ended up in my evaluation, and I was called on the carpet, back at school.

The only thing that saved me was that the same captain had accused another female cadet of the same behavior, in the same cabin, while she was trying to procure the same blueprints. And the only way that even emerged was that she had heard about my story and voluntarily came forward. Ultimately, I was exonerated. The lesson I learned? Appearances matter.

I have had very few noteworthy problems at sea. The few bad experiences, which were very few and very far between, were unpleasant, but not permanently damaging. They are now the stuff of sea stories. I cherish the memories. Rich, saturated, vibrant lives are rarely cultivated by easy circumstances. A life of pleasantness and ease would, indeed, be rather dull.

In my mother's day, a fresh grope was met with a swift slap. Not that I'm advocating slapping, but what man with any testosterone is going to run to his boss and say that a girl slapped him?

When I was groped or grabbed, I usually dealt with it on the spot by threatening the fellow, in my most colorful sailor's tongue, with some sort of gruesome bodily harm. If the behavior continued, I would approach my supervisor, but except for one case I'm about to share with you, the mild harassment I experienced never escalated to that point.

Rather than sneer at winks, sexual innuendo, and romantic suggestions, I would often counter by complimenting the fellow on his *extraordinary* good taste in women, and inform him that, unfortunately, I was spoken for—even if I was single. I'd smile and explain that if he had just reached me sooner, who knows what might have blossomed—but that for now, I was taken. This usually left everyone in good humor, as it allowed the man to save face. When my usual deflections failed (which was rare), I had the occasional mild scuffle. They were brief, usually ending with my eyes fiercely locked with those of my foe, and him backing away.

In the modern workplace, any unwelcome touching is best brought to the attention of a supervisor so that a paper trail may be initiated, in case the harassment doesn't stop and the perpetrator needs to be disciplined. Many companies have policies requiring you to notify the offending party first, and then bring the situation to a superior if the offensive behavior persists. If notification from you proves ineffective, a warning from a supervisor should stop the bad behavior.

In my case, not complaining to the captain about every flirtation often endeared me to the rest of the crew, and they would put the screws to any guy who bothered me. I believe too many women are taught to detonate a bomb, rather than cleverly defuse it. It was usually most effective for me if I could curtail the offensive behavior privately, and let the guy save face. Granted, with my razor-sharp tongue, my youthful arrogance, and my sturdy physique, I wasn't exactly low-hanging fruit.

There was this one time I stabbed a guy. It really was more of a "pricking" and was purely unintentional, but it still counts. I was young and pretty. A crewman on my watch kept flirting with me. My usual deflections weren't working and his advances became relentless. He started touching me, patting my hand, brushing my arm if it was nearby, and making inappropriate gestures. One day he made it hard for me to pass him in a narrow passageway without brushing against him.

After scraping by, I wheeled around and told him, reaching for the Leatherman® tool on my belt, that if he continued this crap, I'd cut off his giblets—or words to that effect. He apparently wasn't too worried about being turned into a soprano, because the next day he crossed the line by grabbing my rear end.

The next watch, I took the ship off the iron mike (the auto-pilot), the normal steering mode, once safely out to sea. Instead, I put my assailant in hand-steering for the rest of the trip. This upset him, and he groused and grumbled every time he was at the helm. He whined and asked why I had done such a mean thing. I politely informed him that he obviously needed something to do with his hands, other than grope me, so I decided he could use them to steer. He didn't touch me again and the flirting stopped, so I figured the issue had been resolved.

It was well into the 00x04 bridge watch one dark morning, and I had the blackout curtain pulled around the chart table as I leaned over it—I'm short—plotting our position. The crewman left the wheel, quietly slipped in behind the curtain and pressed into me from behind, startling me. I was holding a pair of heavy, old-fashioned brass dividers, the really pointy kind. I spun around, and without meaning to, I sort of stuck him in the ribs—rather firmly, by all appearances.

Well, between the blood on the guy's white T-shirt and his loud wailing, one would think I had disemboweled him. Grabbing his side, he went plunging down the stairs to the old man's cabin and pounded on the door. I could hear the pounding in the wheelhouse, two decks up. When the captain opened the door, this crewman blurted out, "The third mate stabbed me!" Needless to say, the phone on the bridge rang almost instantly. I explained to the captain, as best I could, why I had "stabbed" this poor man.

Groping or grabbing anyone aboard ship is a serious violation of the Code of Federal Regulations. Well, so is stabbing, but I was exonerated, as it was in self-defense and truly was an accident. With minimal persuasion, the randy young lad was more than willing to quit the ship at the next port.

After he'd gone, several of the crew came up, congratulated me, and asked why I hadn't stabbed him sooner. Hindsight is twenty-twenty.

Even better, though, by the time the story made its way to the union halls back in the States, it had metamorphosed quite a bit. The new story was that the guy had innocently winked at me and I had chased him down the passageway with a meat cleaver! That may be why I had so few problems in my career. Establish your reputation early!

Seriously though, the real lesson here is that my mere presence was a crucial catalyst for this incident. I know it sounds as though I'm blaming myself for the bad actions of a rude, aggressive man, but you must recognize that having me aboard, through no fault of my own, caused a headache for the captain that night, even if I did succeed in "taking out the trash." After dealing with that experience, could you blame this captain for groaning the next time a woman walked up the gangway? And if she was good-looking, it would only increase his headaches.

So now, when I board a new ship, I do everything I can to put people's minds at ease, and assure them I won't be mortally wounded if a guy gives me a compliment, even if it's crude, or if I hear an off-color joke, or notice a dirty magazine or pornographic movie. This attitude has usually resulted in an almost audible sigh of relief from the whole ship.

I am not advocating tolerating a truly hostile work environment where you are being impeded in your ability to do your job, or enduring unrelenting crude jokes or behaviors that are clearly beyond the pale. I am advocating reason, fairness, balance, and growing a thick skin, to fit into the work environment you chose. Don't expect an industry or military service to change its traditional customs, rhythm, and character, just to suit your particular delicate sensitivities.

9

You're Not in Kansas Anymore:
Going to Town

"Unknown Package" by Stephen C. Coutts

♂♀♂

Going to town may be entirely at your employer's discretion. For mariners and military personnel, going ashore or into town is entirely at the commanding officer's discretion. The captain of a ship has complete control over who goes ashore, for how long, and can even dictate a wandering radius, and/or places his mariners may or may not go and things they may or may not do. Some employers may, because of legal considerations overseas and your status in the host country, have similar rights over you.

When mariners land in a foreign port, they do not have an entry visa. Crew members are allowed to land on foreign soil by virtue of their being signed aboard a vessel as a crew member, and that vessel's having been officially cleared to land in that nation.

No matter how you got to your overseas workplace, you are not a tourist. Usually you must carry some sort of port pass, visa, or other documentation detailing your right to be in the host country.

Whenever going to town, always carry a card written in the local language, listing the address and phone number of your base, ship, or workplace, and information for your designated local contact. It doesn't hurt to carry contact information for the Embassy or Consulate, either. It is the local contact who's likeliest to bail you out of jail if you've been detained by authorities, or to locate you at a hospital.

I was aboard a ship sailing in the Mediterranean and we docked at Alexandria, Egypt. We had two cadets aboard. The deck cadet (from a maritime academy that will remain unnamed) was a blonde, pretty little thing, and she knew it. She wore very short shorts, and walked with a flirty wiggle, giggling at the men. She seemed to enjoy the male attention she was eliciting.

The captain was getting tenser by the day, but was reluctant to confront her. At the time, there were news stories about sex slavery in the Middle East. Apparently blonde women were prized and were being kidnapped. I don't recall whether the disappearances were in Egypt or not, but the captain was concerned. (The rest of us, frankly, wouldn't have missed her.)

He ended up allowing the entire ship's complement ashore, except for her. Her howls of protest could be heard virtually around the globe, as she phoned the academy, the shipping line, her parents, and anyone else who would listen.

This young woman was kept aboard not because of her sex (after all, I was allowed ashore) but because of the immature, unprofessional, and naïve behavior she exhibited aboard this ship.

Know Your Stuff

Never, never, never, ever agree to carry anything the contents of which you do not know and/or can't confirm. In some countries it is a common shakedown for someone who appears to be a local official to lure a young, obviously unseasoned person to carry a package or packet of mail into a facility. At the gate, the guard asks what's in the package, and the unsuspecting employee says it is official mail. The guard then explains that the postman already brought the mail, and demands to open the packet, inside of which, of course, is ambiguous white powder, or some questionable brown sludge, or a leafy substance.

Rather than risk arrest, the employee (if he or she is lucky enough not to be jailed) is asked to pay off the gate guard to keep quiet. Sometimes a mock official will even extract a fine from the employer to resolve things quickly and quietly. It's not as though the employer can simply ring up a local attorney or ask law enforcement to straighten things out.

Regardless of the outcome, the situation at best disrupts the workplace or delays the ship, which is costly.

If you are jailed, almost all ships will just depart without you and a land-based employer may just let you rot. All this and it probably was only baking powder.

Follow the Host Country's Laws

Once you are in a foreign country, their laws apply. When I was a cadet, a story made its way back to the U.S. about two drunken male cadets who decided that peeing on a flagpole sounded like a good idea. (I am not sure why it is men feel they have to pee *on* something, rather than just pee, but pee on the flagpole they did.) This flagpole happened to be in Turkey. The same incident in the U.S. would have landed the kids in county jail, maybe for one night at worst. Perhaps they would have been subjected to a severe finger wagging.

The Turks saw things a little differently. It is my understanding the academy had to pull quite a few strings to secure their release. I don't know whether the story is true or not, but I shudder to imagine what spending even one night in a Turkish jail would be like. Don't test the tolerance of foreign officials.

Money Changing

I was on a break-bulk ship off-loading "give-away grain" in the city of Maputo, Mozambique (a city formerly known as Lorenzo Marques). We were alongside for over a month, since the corn was mostly offloaded by sling and hand, a long, drawn-out process. I had the 00x08 cargo watch. On one of my afternoons off, I made my way to the local market, about a mile from the ship.

Rather than change my money at the bank, which would have been a very long walk in the unforgiving African sun, I decided to barter directly with the merchants, using a combination of goods and dollars, the internationally accepted currency. At other ports, this had always secured a better exchange rate than changing money at banks or street-side money changers. (Nowadays, the best exchange rates are often found at ATMs.)

I finished my shopping and, laden with bags of souvenirs, toiletries, and some hair bands, I made my way back to the ship.

The gate guard was a big, burly, and well armed local woman. As I walked up to the gate, she asked to see my receipts. I explained as best I could that I had shopped at the local market and had no receipts. She became agitated and, after a few rough gesticulations and jabs at my bags and purse, I came to understand she needed to see the receipt from where I had changed my money. Of course I didn't have one, since I hadn't used a bank.

This resulted in her bracing me up, with her AK-47 to my throat, accusing me of illegal money changing. I guess I had broken a law requiring all money be changed at a bank. I got out of it by offering her one of the bottles of shampoo I had bought for myself. She wasn't interested in any of the carvings. The lesson here: know the local laws.

Local Dress Codes

Another area which warrants special consideration when overseas is local dress codes. In some countries, bare ankles or elbows, while not illegal, may signal that you are a prostitute, or at least very available. In some countries, grabbing a woman's breast is considered a compliment. I know this after having been to Italy on a container ship where just making my way down the deck was a virtual obstacle course, between all the longshoremen. Research the countries you plan on visiting and ask questions of others who have been there.

Eating and Drinking Ashore

Ideally, you should never go into town alone, and definitely never eat or drink alone. Depending on the country, the water may not be safe to drink, and raw or undercooked foods may not be safe to eat. In general, avoid uncooked fish and rare meats; don't eat anything you can't peel yourself; and don't necessarily trust that bottled water is truly pure and in its original container, especially in third-world countries. It is all too easy for an unscrupulous merchant to refill a bottle and glue the top band on, so that it looks new. We have had cadets fall ill from third-world "bottled water."

Usually canned or bottled sodas (as distinguished from fountain drinks) and other beverages that are less easily counterfeited are the real thing. Be alert also to the possibility of so-called date-rape drugs being slipped into drinks or food. Again, it's always best to go into town with someone else. Just be prudent and you should be fine.

Bad Parts of Town

If I was in a country where I had to walk through rough neighborhoods just to get into town, I might not bother going. It depends. Ports, refineries and bases are usually not in the best parts of town. Be aware that in many places, just a block either way can make a huge difference. Always have your wits about you and your antenna up. Don't dull your senses and reflexes by getting buzzed or drunk. I can't tell you how many cadets I have seen come back to the ship after having been mugged right after they left a bar. If you were a thug, wouldn't you hang out there? One young man returned to the ship wearing nothing but a tablecloth and a welt the size of a banana on his head.

I advise removing watches, jewelry (expensive or not), and anything else that might make you an attractive target. Even if the jewelry or watch is essentially worthless, the bad guys don't know this.

Your rights to self-defense vary from country to country, just as they do between states in the U.S. For example, in the majority of states, but not all, permits shall be issued to average, law abiding citizens allowing them to carry a firearm canceled on their person. Some states don't allow the carriage of batons or bats for self-defense, while others do. Some states require that victims try to run away from an attacker before defending themselves; others allow self-defense immediately upon an attack.

If you are going in to a foreign town, before carrying pepper spray or a knife in your purse, ensure you know the local laws, as carrying such weapons could land you in jail.

Taxicabs

Taxis can be both a blessing and a curse. In some ports, there have been instances where a taxi driver detoured down a narrow residential road only to be stopped by a band of thugs who would rob the passengers—sometimes at gunpoint. Some believe that, in shake-downs like this, the taxi driver is often part of the hold-up gang. I suspect this is more likely than not, considering that any

"Danger at the Docks" by Michael J. Durnan

good taxi driver would know to avoid the bad parts of town—if he wanted to.

Another problem with taxis in some ports is that they are not metered, or the rates change after dark or on weekends, or the rates change based on the number of riders, or their bags, etc. Before you get in, negotiate the price and make sure you have enough to pay the driver. It is also crucial to have your destination written on a little card in the local language. This is especially true for women, as many cab drivers will find it implausible that an unescorted woman would want to be dropped off at the local cargo pier, refinery, or military base, especially after dark. I have actually found myself arguing with taxi drivers who refused to take me to the port because it was "too dangerous for a woman."

In some countries, if a taxicab is involved in an accident, the rider is held responsible. This is more common in the Middle East than in other parts of the world. Ask the agent or others who have visited the port before to explain the intricacies of the local taxicabs. Don't assume they have your welfare at heart.

Trust Your Guts

In the past, I have allowed the siren song of powerful intellectual and social conditioning to drown-out the tiny voice of my gut instincts. Almost every time I have ignored or overruled a gut instinct, I have regretted it. If, at any time, something just doesn't feel right, heed your instincts. To emphasize the importance of following one's gut instincts, in my simulation classes I tell a tale of a woman getting into an elevator late at night, with a seedy looking fellow. Her guts were firing off warnings and she was apprehensive, but her intellect and social conditioning told her "not to judge a book by its cover" so, not wanting to appear "discriminatory", she boarded the elevator anyway. There isn't a dog, cat, lion, or cockroach that would have boarded that elevator. Trust your instincts.

Final Thoughts

"Time" by Michael J. Durnan

♂♀♂

Never forget that there are stupid and mean people everywhere. People may pick on you not just because you're a girl, but because you're pretty, new, ugly, smart, tall, young, stupid, short, fat, old, skinny, a redhead, blonde, or freckled—just like in grade school.

Recognize that different cultures place different values on things like sanitation, honesty, equality, and fair dealing. For example, in many countries not only is bribery legal, it is expected. Don't expect people of other countries, cultures, or generations to think like you do or share your values.

When a significant person suggests something, it is rarely a mere suggestion. Usually it is a test, or a sounding out. Not a test of your skills, but a measure of your commitment and enthusiasm. I often generate extra-credit exam questions from suggested, but non-required reading. This usually highlights the best students. A supervisor may make a suggestion and watch carefully who acts on the hint.

My husband graduated with honors from Husband School. If I merely hint that some fresh flowers would be nice for the house, he inevitably shows up with a bouquet the next day. Respond to suggestions as if they were instructions. This shouldn't be drudgery. If it is, you're in the wrong place—or the wrong relationship.

The key to a joyous, satisfying life is finding work in which extra effort is fun. Fulfillment lies in getting paid for an activity you would gladly perform until the wee hours of the morning.

If you have no idea what you are meant to do, look at your bookshelf. Evaluate the type of magazines you enjoy. Consider how you spend your free time. How do you like to dress? What types of people do you enjoy?

It doesn't make sense to work fifty weeks a year, in order to earn just two weeks to do what you really enjoy. I have never liked that ratio, nor have I ever worked it.

In the U.S. you have the freedom to pursue your passion. You are not limited by class, race, gender, religion, or the place of your birth. If you have no burning passion, do something worthy and let life's eddies nudge you towards your destination. Don't just be a stick floating down life's river. Be a stick with an engine, a rudder, and someone at the helm!

I hope you will pursue your goals, and take risks to get where you want to be. Most people regret the things they *didn't* do. The number of options available and choices to be made in life can be daunting. Don't worry if you don't know what you're supposed to do with your life. I didn't find my calling until I was in my mid-thirties.

Reflecting on my life and observing the behaviors of young people, I have come to believe there are two kinds of mistakes people make: life-changing mistakes and life-inhibiting mistakes. A life-changing mistake is one you cannot undo or repair. Life-inhibiting mistakes are those you may be able to repair, but they waste time and/or money.

As a college teacher, the most common life-changing events I hear about include having unwanted or poorly timed children, earning a criminal record, or catching a sexually-transmitted disease.

The most common life-inhibiting mistakes I observe are people staying in unfulfilling jobs and/or relationships. Unless a person is saving money for a specific goal, a high-paying but unfulfilling job ultimately will leave him or her frustrated and unhappy. For me, I knew I had to quit going to sea the day I stared out at an empty, gray ocean, and decided I had been everywhere I wanted to go. I realized I was just trading blocks of time for cash, and I had to make a change.

Most of my life-inhibiting decisions, which cost me time and money, involved poor-quality personal relationships. I stayed in adequate but stagnant relationships because they were comfortable and better than being alone, or so I thought. I usually picked men with whom I could remain safely in control. My parents were frustrated with my choices and felt I could "do so much better." What I wasn't able to articulate, was that I didn't *want* to "do better." I picked exactly what I thought I needed for each stage of my life. My actions in relationships were often selfish and failed to propel me graciously through life. I regret that I was so slow to learn this.

Since I had no real direction, I didn't have a sense that I was wasting time. Most young people, not knowing yet what they want in life, have no defined goals, thus no time limits and no sense of urgency. Time becomes something to kill, not to treasure.

I wasted a lot of time in my twenties. I jaunted about the planet, worked hard, and relished my adventures. I was having fun, but I was aiming nowhere and creating nothing of lasting value. I was a ship underway, but without a destination. And for a ship with no destination, any course will do.

In my late twenties, my perspective on intimacy and relationships changed forever. I was living with a nice, but inappropriate guy. One day, he wanted to go to the store but had no cash. He asked to borrow my ATM card, and I wouldn't give him my PIN.

We didn't fight over this—we just stood there looking at each other. It hit me like a sledgehammer: I was giving my time and my body to someone to whom I wouldn't even entrust my PIN!

I realized how little I valued myself. I realized that as a live-in girlfriend, I was doing all the domestic duties of a wife. But I didn't enjoy the security, the social status, or the legal rights that accrue only through marriage. I realized my boyfriend's domestic workload had shrunk to zero, while mine had doubled!

In that instant, I matured and a weight was lifted off me. Everything became clear. I decided never to live with a man to whom I wasn't married, and never to be intimate with anyone to whom I wouldn't give all my worldly possessions.

I encourage you to be really honest with yourself. Cherish your body and your time. Don't waste either in a job or relationship that is merely adequate. Life is too short.

"No Way!" by Stephen C. Coutts

As you make your way through life, focus on contributing to the universe and making each place better for your having been there. Honor and respect the planet, your country, and yourself.

I wish you all the adventure and joy that life has to offer, and I hope you will learn from my mistakes. I have had more excitement and adventure than most people have in a lifetime. I had wonderful, extraordinary experiences working in "a man's world." With the right skills and attitude, you will too!

Endnotes

1   Mercy Wright, e-mail message to author; January 11, 2010.

2   Aboard a commercial ship there is a display frame mounted in a passageway called a "license rack", on which officers are required to publicly display their licenses as long as they are serving aboard the vessel. Having one's license "in the rack" means one is officially serving as an officer aboard a ship.

3   See note 1 above.

4   Women's Bureau of the U.S. Department of Labor's official Web site, http://www.DOL.gov/wb/factsheets/nontra2008.htm.

5   Roseann Richard, *The Perceptions of Women Leaders in Law Enforcement on Promotions, Barriers and Effective Leadership,* (UMI Dissertation Services, 2001), 74-76.

6   Pat Winter, in discussion with the author; January 3, 2010, Benicia, California.

7   Eric Hoover. "Federal Court Strikes Down University's Civility Policy as Basis for Discipline." *San Francisco Chronicle* (November 8, 2007). http://Chronicle.com/article/Federal-Court-Strikes-Down/39913.

8   "Leaders," *The Economist*, January 2nd-8th, 2010, 7.

9   Helen Kennedy, "Former NASA astronaut Lisa Nowak escapes jail with plea deal in violent love triangle case," *New York Daily News* (November 10, 2009). http://www.NYDailyNews.com/news/national/2009/11/10/2009-11-10_former_astronaut_lisa_nowak_.html.

10   For excellent lists of meaningful books, consider visiting http://www.RandomHouse.com, http://www.Time.com/time/2005/100books, and http://www.Newsweek.com/id/204478.

11   The poem goes:

> For want of a nail, the shoe was lost.
> For want of a shoe, the horse was lost.
> For want of a horse, the rider was lost.
> For want of a rider, the battle was lost.
> For want of a battle, the kingdom was lost.
> And all for the want of a horseshoe nail.

Reportedly, this poem was first printed in England in John Gower's *Confessio Amantis*, circa 1390.

12   For an excellent on-line synopsis of basic table manners and other protocol, consult: http://www.CuisineNet.com/glossary/tableman.html and http://www.MannersInternational.com/. Also available are numerous books on the subject, including *Etiquette,* by Emily Post (William Morrow, 2004), *The Amy Vanderbilt Complete Book of Etiquette,* by Amy Vanderbilt (Doubleday, 1995), and *Miss Manners' Guide to Excruciatingly Correct Behavior, Freshly Updated*, by Judith Martin and Gloria Kamen (W.W. Norton & Co., 2005). I also recommend *Please Don't Drink from the Finger Bowl!™*, by Pat Mayfield (ProfessorSales.com, 2005), a small book focused on behaviors in a business setting.

13   Immunization recommendations are posted on various government Web sites, such as those of the U.S. Centers for Disease Control and Prevention, at http://www.CDC.gov and the U.S. State Department, at http://www.state.gov.

14   See note 1 above.